THE REAL
Japanese Izakaya
COOKBOOK

120 Classic Bar Bites from Japan

WATARU YOKOTA

Foreword by **MAKIKO ITOH**

TUTTLE Publishing
Tokyo | Rutland, Vermont | Singapore

CONTENTS

Foreword

DISCOVER the FOODS the JAPANESE really eat EVERYDAY!

An izakaya is an informal pub or bar in Japan. Every town, big or small, has at least a few izakaya. There are big, loud and raucous ones, as well as quiet hole-in-the-wall places down narrow back alleys. Besides being places to have an adult beverage or two, izakaya are known for their *otsumami*, small plates of delicious food that go really well with your drinks. These plates are designed for sharing, tapas-style, with your companions.

   In this book, Chef Wataru Yokota shows you how to make many classic, widely popular izakaya dishes at home, while also adding his unique twists. Most of the ingredients are easy to source. Others may be more of a challenge to find, but that can be part of the fun—discovering new tastes! All the recipes are presented in clear, easy steps. It's a great introduction to this unique and fun genre of Japanese cuisine. Why not recreate an izakaya in your home?

Makiko Itoh
Author of *The Just Bento Cookbook*

Introduction

The BEST IZAKAYA in TOWN is at HOME

Whether you're enjoying a regular nightcap or entertaining guests, or simply giving yourself a pat on the back for getting through another long day, make it a special occasion with a delicious Japanese izakaya-style meal.

In this book you'll find recipes for a range of izakaya fare. Some are straight-up versions of Japanese favorites, some are old favorites with a new twist, some are more adventurous recipes for those who relish a challenge. In other words, you'll find a broad variety of options that can be prepared for any scenario.

On weekday evenings after a busy day at work, you can just make two to three quick snacks. On weekends, when you have more time, you can try one of the more complicated dishes. Or you can assemble an entire menu to entertain guests. Try putting together your own unique combinations, based on what you have on hand, how you feel that day, and who you are dining with.

With these delicious snacks and drinks, your own home becomes the best izakaya in town. Because you're at home, you don't need to feel constrained by any rules regarding the types of drinks you're having to accompany your food—you're free to please yourself. And in the process you may even discover some new and unexpected food-and-drink combinations that really work.

At the end of an evening of relaxed drinking and snacking, be sure to finish things off in true izakaya style with a *shime*, or final course, from the last chapter of this book. After a comforting rice, noodle or pasta dish, you can close up your personal izakaya for the night with body and soul fulfilled and contented, ready to tackle a new day tomorrow.

Wataru Yokota

GOOD to KNOW: Some BASICS

In this section, learn how to make dashi stock and other basic techniques.

HOW TO MAKE DASHI STOCK

Dashi stock is one of the building blocks of Japanese cuisine. Many Japanese use instant dashi stock powder (which is available in most supermarkets worldwide). And that's fine for most of the recipes in this book. But for a truly authentic taste, try making your own dashi stock from scratch. This quick and easy version is made by simmering kombu seaweed and bonito flakes together.

MAKES ABOUT 2 CUPS (500 ML)

1 piece dried kombu seaweed, about
    7 x 4 in (18 x 10 cm) (see note,
    page 11)
1¼ cups (15 g) bonito flakes
    (see note, page 11)
2 cups (500 ml) water

1 Wipe off the surface of the kombu seaweed with a damp kitchen towel.
2 Put the water and kombu in a pan over high heat.
3 When small bubbles start to form on the surface of the water at the

sides of the pan, and the kombu begins to float (about 175°F/80°C), add all the bonito flakes in one go, push them into the water and lower the heat to medium.
4 Remove any surface scum, turn the heat down to low and simmer for an additional 3 minutes. Keep the heat very low, so that the surface of the liquid just gently heaves occasionally. Turn off the heat and let the pan sit for 1 minute, until the bonito flakes sink to the bottom.
5 Pass the liquid through a sieve lined with a thick paper towel. Lightly squeeze out the paper towel afterward to extract a little extra liquid.

To Store Dashi Stock
Cool the dashi stock down completely before transferring to an airtight container. It will keep in the refrigerator for 2 days, and in the freezer for about 3 weeks. To store dashi stock in the freezer, it's even more convenient to pour it into ice trays, freeze and store the cubes in a resealable plastic bag.

HOW TO SHRED CABBAGE
Peel the cabbage leaves off the head one by one. Stack the leaves, roll them up, and slice thinly from the edge.

HOW TO SLICE CUCUMBER INTO MATCHSTICKS
Slice the cucumber thinly on the diagonal. Stack up 4 to 5 slices so that each slice is slightly offset from the one below it. Slice into matchsticks.

HOW TO SLICE CARROTS INTO MATCHSTICKS
1 Peel the carrot and cut into thin rounds.
2 Stack up 4–5 slices so that each slice is slightly offset from the one below it. Slice into ⅛-inch (3-mm) wide strips.

HOW TO CUT CARROTS ROUGHLY
Peel the carrot and cut it into half crosswise. Quarter the fat part of the carrot lengthwise. Cut the carrot up into chunks while turning it 90 degrees one way then the other, so that the knife always cuts into it diagonally, making sure that the pieces are all about the same size.

HOW TO CHOP ONIONS

1 Peel the skin and cut off the root end. Slice in half lengthwise. Place one half on the cutting board so that the root end is on the far side and the cut side is facing down. Slice the onion thinly, keeping about 1 in (3 cm) of the root end uncut.

2 Make about 3 cuts into the onion that are perpendicular to the cuts you made in step 1, holding your knife parallel to the cutting board. Make sure not to cut through the attached root end.

3 Make very fine cuts across the cuts made in step 1 down to the root end.

4 Slice the remaining root end about ⅛ inch (3 mm) thick.

5 Finally, hold down the tip of the knife with one hand as you rock the knife back and forth over the chopped onion with the other, to chop it up very finely.

HOW TO CUT A JAPANESE OR BABY LEEK, OR THICK GREEN ONION INTO MATCHSTICKS

This cut is often used to make a garnish in Japanese cooking.

1 Cut the white part of the leek into 2-in (5-cm) lengths. Make one lengthwise cut about halfway through the leek.

2 Remove the core (it can be reserved for use in soups and other dishes). Spread out the rest of the leek and slice very thinly lengthwise.

HOW TO SEGMENT AN ORANGE

1 Slice a little off the top and bottom of the orange and place it end-up on the cutting board. Insert the knife blade between the flesh and the peel and cut away the peel in 6 to 8 pieces.

2 Make a V cut between the flesh and the membrane and remove the segment.

HOW TO MINCE GARLIC

1 Cut the garlic clove in half and remove the shoot in the core. Place the cut side of one half on the cutting board and press down hard on it with the side of your kitchen knife. This will crush it along the fiber of the clove.

2 Chop finely from one end.

3 Hold down the tip of the knife with one hand as you rock the knife back and forth over the garlic to mince it very finely.

USE OLIVE OIL TO MINCE GARLIC
If your recipe calls for both garlic and olive oil, using a little olive oil at the mincing stage will make the job easier. Chop the garlic following steps 1 and 2 left, then add a little olive oil (see photo). Continue finely mincing the garlic as directed in step 3, left.

CLEANING and PREPARING SQUID and FISH

HOW TO CLEAN AND PREPARE A WHOLE SQUID

1 Place the squid on the cutting board with the fin facing up. Insert your fingers into the body and disconnect the parts where the head is attached to the body.
2 Hold the head with one hand as you gently pull out the legs and innards.
3 Remove the transparent quill from the body. Put your fingers inside the body again and remove any remaining innards as you rinse the squid under running water. Pat the squid body dry with paper towels. Cut up the body as directed in the recipe.

WHEN PEELING OFF THE SKIN, REMOVE THE FIN

If the recipe calls for the squid body to be skinned, insert your fingers between the ears (the fin-like parts that stick out from the top of the body) and the body. Peel off the fin. With a paper towel, grab the skin edge that is hanging off the body where the fin was removed, and peel the skin off.

4 To cut up the guts and legs, insert the knife in the depression between the innards and the eyes. Cut through.
5 Insert the knife in between the eyes and slice partially through. Push out both sides and flatten.
6 Remove the hard beak. Make a slanted cut into an eyeball, push it out the cut from the other side and cut off to remove. Repeat with the other eyeball.
7 To prepare the legs, lightly scrape the suckers off with a knife.
8 Cut ¼–½ in (1–2 cm) off the tips of the legs. Cut up the legs as directed in the recipe.

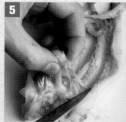

CLEANING and PREPARING a WHOLE FISH

HOW TO CUT OPEN A FISH FROM THE BACK

This method of cutting open a whole fish from the back side, called sebiraki, is used to prepare a variety of fish. I'm demonstrating here with a horse mackerel.

1 Cut off the back fin with kitchen scissors.
2 Lay your knife flat against the base of the tail. Remove the hard spiny part that starts at the tail and runs up the side of the fish, slowly wiggling the knife back and forth under it. Repeat on the other side of the fish.
3 Holding onto a side fin, insert the knife at the base of the head and cut the head off.
4 Turn the fish so that the head end is facing to the right if you're right-handed. Scrape out the innards with the tip of the knife, being careful not to cut through them. Rinse out the body well and pat dry with paper towels.
5 Lay the fish on the board with the back side facing you. Slice through the fish starting from the head end, sliding the blade over the spine, all the way down to the tail.
6 Scrape down the spine so that no flesh remains on it and open up the fish.
7 With the skin side facing up, slice into the fish from the tail end over the spine.
8 Move the blade little by little.
9 Cut into the base of the tail and remove the spine.
10 Remove the bone that is in the depression in the middle of the fish by inserting the knife into the flesh diagonally and scraping it off.
11 Remove the small bones that are lined up in a row in the middle of the flesh using a fish bone tweezer. They are easier to remove if you pull them out in the direction of the head end.

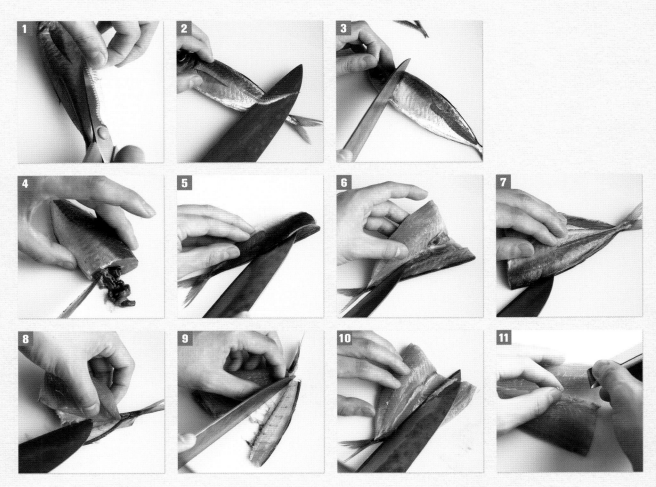

CLEANING and PREPARING SMALL FISH

HOW TO OPEN UP SARDINES WITH YOUR HANDS

This method, called tebiraki in Japanese, is great for quickly preparing small, tender fish like sardines, as demonstrated here.

1 Cut off the back fin with kitchen scissors.
2 Remove the scales by scraping a knife along the fish, starting from the base of the tail. Repeat on the other side.
3 Insert the knife at the base of the head and cut the head off.
4 Place the fish with the head side facing right and the belly facing you if you're right handed. Slice off a 1–1½-in (2.5–4-cm) long strip from the belly side starting from the head end.
5 Open up the belly of the fish and scrape out the innards with the blade of the knife. Wash out the fish

well under running water and pat dry with paper towels.
6 Place the fish on the board with the head end facing you. Push your thumb between the flesh and the spine and open up the fish while sliding your thumb along the spine.
7 Break off the spine at the base of the tail.
8 Hold onto the flesh with one hand, as you slowly remove the spine with the other towards the head end.
9 Remove the bone that is in the depression on both sides of the fish by inserting the knife into the flesh diagonally and scraping it off.
10 Slice a bit off both sides of the fish to clean it up.

ESSENTIAL to KNOW: Key INGREDIENTS

Listed on these two pages are the basic ingredients used to prepare many of the dishes in this book, with information on where to source, how to use, and substitute ingredients.

Bonito Flakes are made from fermented, dried and aged skipjack tuna. An everyday ingredient in Japanese cooking, they are used to make dashi stock, and as a garnish. You can find bonito flakes at any Japanese grocery store or online. They are called katsuobushi in Japanese.

Chikuwa is a kind of fish sausage with a hole running through the center. It is sold already grilled on the outside, so there are wavy brown marks on the surface. It is often used in stews and soups. While it's sold pre-cooked, it's a good idea to heat it through before eating. It can be found in the refrigerated section at Japanese grocery stores.

Chinese Yam is a long root vegetable with pale brown skin and a viscous, slippery texture. It is called nagaimo in Japan, where it is often eaten raw, either cut up or grated. Some people may experience skin irritation when handling it, although they can often ingest it without any problems. If you have a reaction to it when trying to peel or cut it, try holding it with a plastic bag over your hand, or use rubber gloves. Chinese yam can be found at Chinese, Korean and Japanese grocery stores.

Daikon Radish is a thick white root vegetable with a spicy flavor and a crunchy texture when raw. When cooked, it becomes quite soft and sweet. Daikon radish is one of the most popular vegetables in Japan, used year-round both raw and cooked. You can find it at Asian grocery stores as well as many regular supermarkets.

Kombu seaweed is the thick, leathery green-brown seaweed used to make dashi or Japanese stock, the foundation of traditional Japanese cuisine. It's also used to add a shot of umami in various recipes. Kombu seaweed is always sold in dried form, and is available at Japanese grocery stores or online.

Lotus Root is the rhizome of the lotus plant. The holes running through it give slices an attractive lacy appearance. You'll find it at most Asian grocery stores.

Mentaiko is salted spicy cod or pollack roe. It is a popular filling for onigiri rice balls, and is used often as a condiment. You can find mentaiko at well-stocked Japanese grocery stores, where it is usually sold frozen. Defrost in the refrigerator and use the same day.

Mirin is a sweet alcoholic liquor made from rice, used almost exclusively for cooking. It is so sweet that it's often used instead of sugar in various recipes. A staple in any Japanese kitchen, it can be found in most Asian markets.

Miso is a fermented paste made with soy beans, salt, and Aspergillus oryzae microbes. Grains are often added to the mix—usually wheat, rice or barley—before fermenting. The color of miso can range from a pale yellow brown to a deep reddish brown, almost black. Miso is one of the staples of the Japanese kitchen.

Myoga is a type of ginger bud often used as a garnish. If you can't find myoga, use thinly sliced mature ginger or fresh ginger shoots, which you may be able to find at Chinese or Thai grocery stores.

Panko is simply the Japanese word for breadcrumbs, but in the English-speaking world, the word has come to mean a specific type of large, spiky dried breadcrumb. In this book, some recipes call for spiky panko, others for soft breadcrumbs. The type is clearly specified in each recipe.

Rice Vinegar is the standard type of vinegar used in Japanese cooking. You can find it in Japanese grocery stores as well as many regular supermarkets these days. Take care not to use sushi vinegar instead of rice vinegar, since sushi vinegar may have salt and sugar added to it. Check the label to be sure.

Sake is often used in Japanese recipes to add depth and eliminate off flavors in fish, poultry and meat. You can use cooking sake, available at Japanese grocery stores, or just use a little of the sake you drink.

Satsuma-age is a deep-fried cake made of fish paste and vegetables that is sold ready to eat. It's used in stews and stir-fries or eaten as-is. Chikuwa and satsuma-age can be found in the refrigerated section at Japanese grocery stores.

Sesame Oil is available in Japanese and Asian grocery stores, as well as many regular supermarkets. For Japanese cooking, unless specified otherwise, you should always used the dark, toasted type of sesame oil, not the light-colored one available at some health-food stores.

Shio Koji is used as a marinade in many Japanese dishes. It is made with salt, water and rice koji—rice that has been inoculated with Aspergillus oryzae, a type of beneficial microbe that's used to ferment miso, soy sauce, and sake. Shio koji helps to increase the umami in food; it also tenderizes proteins such as chicken and meat. Shio koji is available at well-stocked Japanese grocery stores in jars or squeeze bottles. You can also make your own using dehydrated rice koji, salt and water. Rice koji is available online from brewing supply companies.

Shiso Leaves (Perilla frutescens var. crispa) are widely used in Japanese cooking. Don't confuse shiso with kkae (Perilla frutescens), which is Korean perilla. Kkae looks similar but has an aniseed-like flavor and fragrance. Kkae has leaves with scalloped edges and purple-tinged undersides, whereas shiso leaves are a lighter green with spiky edges, and are often ruffled. You can find shiso at a well-stocked Japanese grocery store; it's also fairly easy to grow from seed. It's considered a perennial in US zones 10 and 11 and grows as an annual elsewhere.

Soy Sauce is a staple of the Japanese kitchen. Unless specified otherwise, the soy sauce used in this book is regular dark (reddish brown-black) soy sauce. Use a Japanese brand if possible, since soy sauce flavors do vary depending on which country they come from.

Tofu The Western product labeled "firm silken tofu" is suitable for the recipes in this book that call for tofu. One recipe calls for yaki-dofu—this is firm tofu that has been grilled, so it has a slightly firmer texture than regular firm tofu. Yaki-dofu can be found at Japanese grocery stores.

Umeboshi are salt-preserved *ume* plums, which are related to apricots but much more tart. There are two main types of umeboshi: one has soft flesh, and can be chopped up into a paste to use as a seasoning; the other, called *kari-kari ume* in Japanese, is crunchy. Both types of umeboshi (sometimes just abbreviated to "ume") are available at Japanese grocery stores.

Yaki-dofu see Tofu

Yuzu is a type of Japanese citrus. If you can't find it at a Japanese grocery store, use lemon or lime instead.

How to use this book
- One tablespoon is 15 ml, and 1 teaspoon is 5 ml.
- A 600-watt microwave oven was used throughout this book. If the wattage of your microwave varies, please adjust the cooking time accordingly. For instance, if you have a 500-watt microwave, increase the time by 1.2. Cooking times may vary depending on the manufacturer and model of the microwave. Check the owner's manual or the serial plate inside your microwave for the wattage.
- Natural salt processed using traditional methods, and dark (regular) Japanese soy sauce are used.
- Unsalted butter is used in all recipes calling for butter. If you use salted butter instead, decrease the amount of salt in the recipe.
- The flour used in this book is low-gluten or cake flour.

Choosing and Serving Japanese Sake

There are four main varieties of sake:

Ginjo-shu Sake made with white rice that has a rice-polishing ratio* of less than 60 percent, rice koji (rice inoculated with the *Aspergillus* mold used for fermentation), water and brewing alcohol. It often has a fruity or flowery flavor.

Junmai-shu Sake made with white rice, rice koji, and water. As the name (which means "pure rice") indicates, it's made with rice only. It has a heavy, full flavor.

Honjozo-shu Sake made with white rice that has a rice-polishing ratio of less than 70 percent, rice koji, water, and brewing alcohol. It is light, dry, and easy to drink.

Futsu-shu means "ordinary sake," a term used for all sake types other than those above.

*The rice-polishing ratio indicates how much of the bran surrounding the rice grain has been polished off. A rice polishing ratio of 60 percent means that 40 percent of the surface of the rice has been removed.

Temperature
Sake is served at different temperatures depending on the food and the season. *Yuki-bie* (snow-chilled) is 40°F (5°C); *hana-bie* (flower-chilled) is 50°F (10°C); *ryo-bie* (refreshingly chilled) is 60°F (15°C); *jo-on* (room temperature) is 68°F (20°C); *nuru-kan* (lukewarm) is 04°F (40°C); *jo-kan* (warm) is 113°F (45°); and *atsu-kan* (hot) is 122°F (50°C). To heat sake, pour it into a traditional flask (see photo on page 1) and place the flask in a pan of hot water. The water should reach the neck of the flask. Heat the water over low heat until the sake reaches the desired temperature.

Chapter 1

SNACKS and STARTERS

This chapter contains easy-to-make snacks that you can rustle up quickly to accompany the first drink of the evening. These include dishes you mix together, grill or pan-fry. You can prepare many of them in advance and have them ready to serve, making your home izakaya even more efficient! Standard izakaya fare like Chilled Tofu with Toppings, Steam-Fried Edamame, or Cucumber with Sweet Miso keep well in the refrigerator. The following pages contain recipes for classic izakaya favorites such as Pickled Fried Eggplant, Yuzu Marinated Turnips, and Crispy Deep-Fried Tofu with Salted Squid. You'll find some original twists too, like Chikuwa Fish Cake and Olive Pinchos and Thai-Style Salad. Cheers!

MOZUKU SEAWEED in VINEGAR SAUCE

Mozuku seaweed is packed with fiber and other nutrients. You may be able to find it fresh at Japanese grocery stores, or buy it dried online.

SERVES 2

1-in (3-cm) length Chinese yam (see note, page 11)
Piece Japanese or baby cucumber, about 2 oz (60 g)
Small knob fresh ginger
2 oz (60 g) mozuku seaweed, fresh or reconstituted
   (see note, above)

FOR THE VINEGAR SAUCE
3 tablespoons rice vinegar
1 tablespoon sugar
1 tablespoon soy sauce

1 Peel the yam and cut into ¼-in (6-mm) cubes. Cut the cucumber into ¼-inch (6-mm) cubes. Peel the ginger and cut into very fine strips.
2 Combine the vinegar sauce ingredients in a bowl and mix.
3 Put the mozuku seaweed in a serving bowl with the vinegar sauce. Top with the yam, cucumber and ginger.

CHILLED TOFU with TOPPINGS

Cook the sauce in the microwave to give it a rounded, mild flavor.

SERVES 2

2 myoga ginger buds (see note, page 11)
½ sweet onion
2 green onions (scallions)
1 piece silken (kinugoshi) tofu, about 12 oz (350 g)
A handful of bonito flakes (see note, page 11)

FOR THE SAUCE
2 teaspoons peeled and finely chopped fresh ginger
2 tablespoons soy sauce
1 tablespoon mirin (see note, page 11)

1 Put the sauce ingredients in a microwave-safe bowl, cover loosely with plastic wrap and microwave for about a minute. Take out and leave to cool.
2 Thinly slice the myoga and sweet onion lengthwise. Discard the white part of the green onions and slice the greens into thin rounds.
3 Use a spoon to scoop the silken tofu into a serving bowl. Top with the myoga, onion, sliced green onions and bonito flakes.

BOILED POTATOES with NORI SEAWEED BUTTER

Add some ground pink peppercorns for their refreshing fragrance and spicy punch.

SERVES 2

2 potatoes
Pinch of salt
1 tablespoon nori seaweed paste (see note, page 76)
1 teaspoon unsalted butter
1 teaspoon ground pink peppercorns

1 Peel and cut the potatoes in half, then cut the halves into thirds. Put the potato pieces in a colander and rinse briefly under running water.
2 Put the potatoes in a pan with the salt and enough cold water to cover. When the water comes to a boil, lower the heat and simmer for about 10 minutes. When a skewer goes through a potato piece easily, drain the potatoes into a colander and shake well to get rid of the water.
3 Put the nori seaweed paste and butter in a bowl, add the cooked potatoes while they are still hot, and mix well. Arrange on a serving dish and sprinkle with the pink peppercorns.

CHIKUWA FISH CAKE and OLIVE PINCHOS

Pinchos are tapas-like small plates served in bars in northern Spain—a Spanish izakaya snack! Chikuwa are prepared fish cakes (see note, page 11) The combination of salty and sour flavors here works really well.

6 PIECES; SERVES 2

1 chikuwa grilled fish cake, or Thai fish cake
2 canned anchovy fillets
6 pitted black olives

1 Cut the fish cake lengthwise into 6 strips. Chop the anchovy fillets finely.
2 With the grilled side of a fish cake strip facing up, place an olive at one end and roll the fish cake strip around it. Secure with a skewer or toothpick that has been presoaked in water (this way it won't get burned when you bake it). Repeat with the remaining fish cake pieces and olives.
3 Cover a baking sheet with aluminum foil, and put the wrapped olives on it. Sprinkle each pincho with the chopped anchovies. Bake for about 5 minutes in an oven preheated to 400°F (200°C).

Mozuku Seaweed in
Vinegar Sauce

Boiled Potatoes with
Nori Seaweed Butter

Chilled Tofu with Toppings

Chikuwa Fish Cake and
Olive Pinchos

CHINESE YAM with MENTAIKO

The texture of the crushed Chinese yam and the heat of the spiced roe go really well together.

SERVES 2

3-in (8-cm) length Chinese yam (see note, page 11)
1 tablespoon mentaiko roe (see note, page 11)
2 green shiso leaves (see note, page 12)

1 Peel the yam and cut lengthwise into six pieces. Place the pieces in a plastic bag and bash them into smaller pieces using a rolling pin or similar instrument. Cut into the membrane around the mentaiko sac and scrape out the eggs inside.
2 Mix the yam and mentaiko together in a bowl. Transfer to a serving dish lined with the green shiso leaves.

SAKE-STEAMED CHICKEN with YUZU KOSHO PEPPER

Yuzu kosho is a condiment paste made from ground yuzu citrus peel, chili peppers and salt. It has a spicy, salty and sour flavor that many people find addictive, and gives this dish a flavor you won't forget. Shio koji is a fermented mixture of rice, salt and water, a popular seasoning ingredient in Japan. Both are available at Japanese grocery stores or online.

SERVES 2

4 oz (125 g) chicken tenders
½ teaspoon shio koji (see note, page 12)
½ teaspoon sake
½ teaspoon yuzu kosho pepper (see note, above)

1 Remove any sinew from the chicken tenders and place on a microwave-safe dish. Coat with the shio koji and sake, cover loosely with plastic wrap and microwave for about a minute. Leave to cool with the plastic wrap still on.
2 Shred the cooked chicken coarsely with your hands. Put the chicken in a bowl, add the yuzu kosho and mix. Arrange on a serving dish and serve.

STEAM-FRIED EDAMAME

Edamame are young green soybeans, sold still in their pods (which are not eaten). If you can't find them fresh, they are widely available in frozen form. If using frozen edamame, skip step 1.

SERVES 2

5 oz (140 g) fresh or frozen edamame in their pods (see note, above)
½ teaspoon sea salt for rubbing
1 teaspoon sesame oil
1 tablespoon sake
½ teaspoon sea salt for sprinkling

1 Cut off both ends of each edamame pod using kitchen scissors. Use the ½ teaspoon of salt to rub the pods well. Rinse off the salt and any dirt under running water.
2 Spread the sesame oil around in a frying pan and add the edamame. Stir-fry over medium heat for about 3 minutes.
3 When the edamame are lightly browned, spread them around the frying pan evenly and sprinkle with the sake and the remaining ½ teaspoon of salt. Cover and steam-fry over low heat for about 3 minutes. Take off the lid, raise the heat to medium and shake the pan to evaporate the moisture. Serve.

NARAZUKE PICKLES with CREAM CHEESE

Narazuke is a traditional type of pickle consisting of vegetables such as cucumber or winter melon preserved in sake lees. You can find narazuke pickles in well-stocked Japanese grocery stores.

SERVES 2

4 tablespoons cream cheese
4 tablespoons narazuke pickles, or mild kimchi
¼ teaspoon sea salt, or to taste

1 Put the cheese in a bowl and cream it with a wooden spoon.
2 Cut the narazuke into ¼-inch (6-mm) cubes. Add to the creamed cheese, add the salt and mix well. Serve.

Chinese Yam with Mentaiko

Steam-Fried Edamame

Narazuke Pickles with
Cream Cheese

Sake-Steamed Chicken with
Yuzu Kosho Pepper

SLICED SALAMI and ONION

Enjoy the fresh, crunchy sweetness of onion to its fullest in this little dish. Add black pepper for a spicy accent.

SERVES 2

1 small onion
10 thin slices salami (soft type)
Pinch of sea salt, to taste
Coarsely ground black pepper, to taste

1 Cut the onion in half from root end to tip, then slice thinly lengthwise. Soak in cold water for about 5 minutes and drain well before using.
2 Mix the onion, salami, salt and pepper together in a bowl. Cover with plastic wrap and refrigerate for at least 5 minutes. When the onion becomes a little limp, transfer to a serving plate.

SWEET SPICY MIXED NUTS

These nuts are subtly sweet, salty and spicy. It's really impossible to stop eating them!

SERVES 2

2 teaspoons sugar
½ teaspoon sweet paprika powder
¼ teaspoon coarsely ground black pepper
Pinch red pepper powder or cayenne pepper, to taste
1 teaspoon olive oil
1 cup (120 g) mixed salted nuts

1 Combine the sugar, paprika, black pepper, salt and red pepper powder in a bowl and mix well.
2 Heat the olive oil in a frying pan over low heat. Add the mixed nuts and stir-fry for about 3 minutes.
3 When the nuts have turned golden brown, transfer to a large bowl, sprinkle with the seasoning and mix well. Spread the nuts out onto a tray to cool, and transfer to a serving bowl.

CRISPY DEEP-FRIED TOFU with SALTED SQUID

An unbeatable combination of abura-age (ready-made deep-fried tofu), baked until crispy, with the deep rich umami of ika no shiokara (salted squid). You'll find both of these ingredients at Japanese grocery stores.

SERVES 2

1 piece abura-age fried tofu, about 1 oz (30 g), (see note, above)
2 oz (60 g) *ika no shiokara salted squid (see note, page 118), or 3–4 salted anchovies, chopped

*The saltiness of ika no shiokara varies by manufacturer, so adjust the amount to taste.

1 Cut the fried tofu in half lengthwise, then slice into ½-in (1-cm) wide strips. Spread the strips on a baking sheet lined with aluminum foil and toast in an oven preheated to 400°F (200°C) for about 10 minutes, until lightly browned.
2 Place the toasted tofu strips into a bowl. Add the squid, mix and transfer to a serving bowl.

DRIED SQUID and CELERY with SESAME OIL

Shredded dried squid, called *saki ika* in Japanese, is a popular drinking snack that should be easy to find in your Japanese grocery store. The fragrance of the celery and the richness of the sesame oil are a perfect match.

SERVES 2

Large handful shredded dried squid, soft type (see note, above)
1 stalk celery
2 teaspoons sesame oil
Pinch of sea salt, to taste

1 Cut the squid into bite-sized pieces. Remove the tough strings from the celery stalk and slice thinly diagonally.
2 Combine all ingredients in a plastic bag. Massage together until well mixed, then allow to stand for about 10 minutes until the celery is a bit limp. Remove from bag and arrange on a serving dish.

Sliced Salami and Onion

Crispy Deep-Fried Tofu
with Salted Squid

Sweet Spicy Mixed Nuts

Dried Squid and Celery with
Sesame Oil

CUCUMBER with SWEET MISO

The small, seedless Japanese variety of cucumber works best for this dish.

SERVES 2

1 small Japanese cucumber (or ½ baby cucumber)

FOR THE MISO SAUCE
4½ tablespoons miso paste (barley miso if possible)
2 tablespoons sake
1 teaspoon sugar
1 teaspoon soy sauce

1 Combine the sauce ingredients in a small pan and cook over medium heat, stirring constantly, for about 2 minutes until the sauce has thickened. When it's quite thick, take the pan off the heat and allow to cool.
2 Cut off both ends of the cucumber, then cut lengthwise into six sticks. (Note: if you're not using a Japanese cucumber, you may need to deseed it before cutting into sticks.) Arrange on a plate with the miso sauce.

GRATED CHINESE YAM and OKRA with NATTO

This dish combines three delicious foods that are sticky and slimy, including the fermented soybeans known as natto. Sesame seeds and green shiso leaves add flavor and fragrance.

SERVES 2

4 okra pods
Pinch of sea salt
3-in (8-cm) length Chinese yam (see note, page 11)
4 tablespoons split bean (hikiwari) natto (see recipe headnote, page 86)
2 green shiso leaves (see note, page 12)
1 teaspoon soy sauce
1 teaspoon toasted white sesame seeds

1 Sprinkle the okra with the pinch of salt and rub well. Blanch in boiling water for about 30 seconds. Drain and plunge into cold water, then drain well. Cut off the blossom ends, then slice into ½-in (1-cm) pieces.
2 Peel and then grate the Chinese yam. Discard the shiso stems and shred the leaves finely. Combine the natto and soy sauce in a bowl and mix.
3 Arrange the grated Chinese yam in a bowl and top with the okra and the natto. Sprinkle the sesame seeds and shiso over.

DRIED SQUID with KIMCHI

Use the type of dried squid called *surume* or *atarime* in Japanese, which has a hard, chewy texture. It's a popular drinking snack when grilled lightly and shredded.

SERVES 2

Handful dried squid (see note, above)
½ cup (85 g) Napa cabbage kimchi

1 Use kitchen scissors to cut the squid into pieces roughly ½ x 2 in (1 x 5 cm). Cut the kimchi into ¾-in (2-cm) pieces.
2 Put the squid and kimchi into a plastic bag and mix. Refrigerate 6 to 8 hours or overnight, giving the bag a squeeze two or three times during that time. When the squid is soft, it is ready to serve.

CRUNCHY KIRIBOSHI DAIKON STRIPS with SESAME OIL

Kiriboshi daikon is shredded and dried daikon radish. It's important to rehydrate it by soaking in water just to the point where it's still crunchy.

SERVES 2

¼ cup (10 g) sliced dried shiitake mushrooms (see note, page 89)
⅔ cup (160 ml) water for soaking the mushrooms
2 oz (60 g) dried kiriboshi daikon (see note, above)
2 teaspoons sesame oil
⅓ cup (30 g) roasted soybeans*
1 teaspoon soy sauce

*If you can't find ready-made roasted soybeans (called iri daizu in Japanese), soak ¼ oz (10 g) dried uncooked soybeans in water overnight, drain and dry, and roast in a frying pan over low heat, stirring often, for 20–30 minutes.

1 Soak the shiitake mushrooms in the ⅔ cup of water for 20 minutes. Drain, reserving the soaking water.
2 Put the kiriboshi daikon in a bowl filled with water and wash well. Drain in a colander and leave for about 5 minutes, so that it is softened but still firm.
3 Heat the sesame oil in a frying pan over medium heat. Add the roasted soybeans and the kiriboshi daikon from step 2. Stir-fry for about 3 minutes. When everything is well coated with the oil, add the shiitake mushrooms along with their soaking water and the soy sauce. Stir-fry until the liquid has cooked off, and then transfer to a serving plate.

Cucumber with Sweet Miso

Dried Squid with Kimchi

Grated Chinese Yam and
Okra with Natto

Crunchy Kiriboshi Daikon
Strips with Sesame Oil

FRESH SQUID "NOODLES"

Be sure to obtain squid that is suitable for sashimi or sushi. Sashimi-grade squid can be bought at well stocked Japanese grocery stores or from your fishmonger.

SERVES 2

1 clove garlic
1 red Thai chili pepper
1 green onion (scallion)
2 tablespoons olive oil
4 oz (125 g) raw sashimi-grade squid, pre-cut into strips*
1 heaping tablespoon shio koji (see note, page 12)

*If you can't obtain pre-cut squid, follow the instructions on page 8 to clean and prepare a whole squid. Slice the cleaned body into long thin strips.

1 Slice the garlic clove thinly crosswise. Cut the stem end off the chili pepper, remove the seeds and slice into thin rounds. Discard the white part of the green onion and slice the greens into thin rounds.
2 Pour the olive oil into a frying pan over low heat and add the garlic. When it starts to change color, add the chili pepper. Take the pan off the heat and leave to cool.
3 Combine the squid and shio koji in a bowl and mix. Add the sliced green onion and the infused oil, mix again and arrange in a serving bowl.

SEA BREAM CARPACCIO

Sudachi citrus and soy sauce give this carpaccio a Japanese twist. It goes well with sake or white wine.

SERVES 2

1½ oz (40 g) salt-packed dried wakame seaweed
2 red cherry tomatoes
2 yellow cherry tomatoes
½ red or regular onion
Pinch of sea salt
½ sudachi citrus,* or use ½ yuzu or ½ lime
4 oz (125 g) sashimi-grade sea bream (tai) or other sashimi-grade firm white fish (see note, page 102)

FOR THE DRESSING
½ teaspoon sudachi juice (or yuzu or lime juice)
1 teaspoon soy sauce
1 teaspoon olive oil

*Sudachi is a small green citrus with a refreshing fragrance and flavor. If you can't find it, try substituting a mixture of freshly squeezed lime and grapefruit in the dressing, and use green limes for the garnish.

1 Rinse the wakame seaweed and soak in enough water to cover for 5 minutes to soften. Squeeze out the moisture and cut into 1-in (3-cm) long pieces.
2 Core the tomatoes and cut lengthwise into ¼-in (6-mm) thick slices. Thinly slice the red onion crosswise and place in a bowl. Sprinkle the salt over the onion slices and rub it until they become limp, then squeeze out the excess moisture. Cut the half sudachi into two pieces. If the sea bream is not sliced already, slice it thinly.
3 Arrange all the ingredients from steps 1 and 2 on a plate. Mix the dressing ingredients together and pour over before serving.

KOREAN-STYLE TUNA TARTARE

Yukhoe, a tartare-like dish from Korea, is usually made with raw beef. Here I have used sashimi-quality tuna mixed with ginger, garlic and the spicy Korean paste called gochujang. It's a dish with great depth of flavor.

SERVES 2

6 oz (170 g) sashimi-grade lean tuna (see note, page 102)
2 very fresh or pasteurized eggs
¼ teaspoon white sesame seeds
Radish sprouts, for garnish

FOR THE SAUCE
¼ teaspoon minced fresh ginger
¼ teaspoon minced garlic
1 tablespoon soy sauce
2 teaspoons sesame oil
½ teaspoon gochujang hot pepper bean paste

1 Pat the tuna dry with paper towels. Cut into ½-in (1-cm) cubes. Separate the eggs, reserving the whites for another use.
2 Mix the sauce ingredients in a bowl. Add the tuna and stir to combine. Divide between two serving bowls, sprinkle with the sesame seeds and top each bowl with a raw egg yolk. Garnish with a few radish sprouts.

Generously season the tuna to eliminate any fishiness and increase the umami.

Sea Bream Carpaccio

Korean-Style Tuna Tartare

Fresh Squid
"Noodles"

YUZU MARINATED TURNIPS

Small, tender Japanese turnips are ideal for this delicious dish, but regular baby turnips work well too. Kombu seaweed, sold dried at Japanese grocery stores, adds umami to the marinade. This dish can be made a day in advance.

SERVES 2

Baby turnips, about 2 oz (60 g)
1 piece dried kombu seaweed, about 2-in (5-cm) square (see note, page 11)
Peel from ¼ of a yuzu citrus or small lime (see note, page 12)
¼ teaspoon sea salt, divided

1 Cut the greens off the turnips, leaving about ¾-in (2-cm) of the stem attached. Peel the turnips and slice thinly lengthwise. Wipe the surface of the kombu seaweed with a damp kitchen towel. Cut the yuzu peel into very fine matchsticks.
2 Put the turnips, kombu, yuzu peel and half the salt in a resealable bag and massage well to distribute the salt. Let stand until the turnip slices have turned limp.
3 Chop the turnip greens finely and place in a bowl. Sprinkle the remaining salt over and rub the greens with your hands. When they turn limp, squeeze out any excess moisture. Arrange the turnips and greens together on a serving plate.

QUICK PICKLED NAPA CABBAGE

Use shio koji instead of salt to add a gentle sweetness to this quick vegetable dish. I recommend making it a day in advance.

SERVES 2

2 Napa cabbage leaves
½ red Thai chili pepper, or to taste
2 teaspoons shio koji (see note, page 12)

1 Cut the cabbage into 2-in (5-cm) squares. Cut the stem end from the chili pepper, remove the seeds and slice into thin rounds.
2 Put the cabbage and chili pepper into a resealable bag and add the shio koji. Seal the bag and massage and shake it several times. (If you're making this the day before, you don't have to massage it that much—just shake it lightly and leave it to marinate.) When the cabbage has turned limp, transfer to a serving bowl.

MISO MARINATED EGG YOLKS with CUCUMBER

These marinated egg yolks are thick, creamy and delicious, the perfect accompaniment to crunchy Japanese cucumber.

SERVES 2

⅓ cup (100 g) miso paste
2 raw egg yolks from pasteurized or guaranteed fresh eggs*
½ small Japanese cucumber (or ¼ baby cucumber)

1 Spoon 80% of the miso into a container with an airtight lid. Even out the surface and cover with a piece of cheesecloth. Make two indentations in it with the back of a spoon and place the egg yolks in them. Spread the remaining miso on another piece of cheesecloth and gently place it over the yolks. Close the container and refrigerate overnight at minimum, or up to 3 days.
2 Before serving, slice the cucumber diagonally, then slice into fine matchsticks (see page 6). Arrange on a plate. Remove the egg yolks from the miso and place on top of the cucumber.

*If you have extra eggs, you can make a quick and easy snack. Peel two hard-boiled eggs and put them into a resealable bag with 3½ tablespoons of mentsuyu bottled noodle sauce (the "straight-up" type, not the concentrated sauce). Refrigerate for about 6 hours, turning the bag over from time to time. This makes marinated eggs with a sweet-salty flavor. Try using citrus-based ponzu sauce (available readymade in bottles from Japanese grocery stores) instead of mentsuyu for a refreshing variation.

Yuzu Marinated Turnips

Miso Marinated Egg Yolks with Cucumber

Quick Pickled Napa Cabbage

DASHI STEEPED TOMATO

The umami-packed dashi stock permeates the skinned tomato.

SERVES 2

1 large ripe, sweet tomato
1 okra pod
Pinch of sea salt

FOR THE MARINADE
1 scant cup (200 ml) dashi stock (see page 6)
½ teaspoon sea salt, or to taste
½ teaspoon soy sauce

1 Core the tomato and make a shallow crisscross cut into the skin on the bottom. Bring a pan of water to a boil and blanch the tomato for about 10 seconds, or until the skin starts to peel off. Plunge into ice water, then carefully remove the skin.
2 Cut the stem from the okra as closely as possible and sprinkle the pod with the pinch of salt. Blanch for about 30 seconds, plunge in ice water to cool, and cut in half lengthwise.
3 Combine the marinade ingredients in a bowl. Add the tomato and okra, cover and refrigerate overnight. Transfer to a serving bowl and sprinkle with a little salt.

Peel away the tomato skin carefully, taking care not to mar the flesh.

PICKLED FRIED EGGPLANT

Japanese eggplants are thinner than Western ones; find them—or the similar Chinese variety—at an Asian grocery store or the farmers' market.

SERVES 2

2 small Japanese eggplants, about 8 oz (225 g)
Oil for deep-frying
Pinch of sea salt

FOR THE PICKLING LIQUID
½ red Thai chili pepper, deseeded
2 thin slices of garlic
½ bay leaf, torn in half
4 tablespoons rice vinegar
2 teaspoons sugar
1 teaspoon sea salt, or to taste
½ teaspoon soy sauce

1 Combine the pickling liquid ingredients in a microwave-safe bowl. Cover loosely with plastic wrap and microwave for about a minute.
2 Peel thin strips of skin from the length of the eggplants. Cut the eggplants in half lengthwise. Sprinkle with the salt, leave for about 5 minutes, then pat dry.
3 Heat the frying oil to 355°F (180°C). Add the eggplants and fry for about 2 minutes, turning occasionally. Drain on a paper towel and transfer to a container. Pour the pickling liquid over the eggplants. Place a piece of plastic wrap directly on the eggplants (not over the container), covering them completely. Leave to marinate for about 10 minutes, then arrange on a serving plate.

GRILLED BROAD BEANS

Grilling broad beans in their pods so that they steam cook makes the beans plump and sweet.

SERVES 2

4 large broad bean pods
Sea salt, for sprinking

1 Place a grilling rack or pan over medium heat and place the broad bean pods on it. Grill for about 3 minutes, turning from time to time.
2 When the surface of the pods has turned black, transfer to a serving plate and sprinkle with the salt.

Grill the broad beans over a direct flame until the pods turn black on the surface, so that they cook all the way through. You can also use a grill pan, but a longer grilling time will be needed.

Grilled Broad Beans

Pickled Fried Eggplant

Dashi Steeped Tomato

CHINESE-STYLE MIZUNA SALAD with SESAME DRESSING

The deep-fried onion has a wonderful aroma, as well as a satisfyingly crunchy texture.

SERVES 2

1 bunch mizuna greens or watercress,
    about 4 oz (125 g)
¼ onion
1 tablespoon flour
Oil for deep-frying
Pinch of sea salt, to taste

FOR THE SESAME DRESSING

½ teaspoon toasted white sesame seeds
2 teaspoons sesame oil
2 teaspoons soy sauce
½ teaspoon doubanjiang spicy bean paste
    (see recipe headnote, page 124)
½ teaspoon honey
½ teaspoon rice vinegar

1 Cut the roots off the mizuna and slice the leaves into 3-in (8-cm) lengths. Thinly slice the onion crosswise and sprinkle with the flour. Heat the frying oil to 320°F (160°C), add the onion and fry for 5 minutes. When golden brown, remove from the oil and drain on a paper towel. Sprinkle with the salt.
2 Arrange the mizuna on a serving plate and top with the fried onion. Mix the dressing ingredients together and pour over. Toss well before eating.

SCALLOPS and DAIKON with SESAME and MAYO

Sweet scallops paired with crisp daikon radish makes for an unbeatable combination.

SERVES 2

3-in (8-cm) length daikon radish (see note, page 11)
3–4 cooked scallops, about 2 oz (60 g)
½ teaspoon sea salt
½ teaspoon toasted black sesame seeds
3 tablespoons mayonnaise

1 Peel the daikon and cut into sticks ¼ x 2 in (5 mm x 5 cm). Place in a bowl, sprinkle with the salt, and rub with your hands. Let stand for about 5 minutes and then drain off any excess moisture.
2 Shred the scallops coarsely by hand into a large bowl. Add the salted daikon, the sesame seeds and the mayonnaise. Mix well and transfer to a serving dish.

IZAKAYA POTATO SALAD

Potato salad is another classic izakaya snack. This version has ham, cucumber and onion added to the potatoes. It tastes so good because it's so simple!

SERVES 2

2 potatoes
Pinch of salt
1 tablespoon rice vinegar
3 slices smoked ham
⅓ Japanese cucumber, or small piece baby cucumber
¼ onion
4 tablespoons mayonnaise
¼ teaspoon sea salt

1 Peel the potatoes and cut in half, then cut each half into 4 pieces. Rinse in a colander under running water and drain well.
2 Place the potatoes in a pan with enough cold water to cover and the pinch of salt. Bring to a boil, then lower the heat and simmer for about 10 minutes. When a skewer pierces the potato easily, drain into a colander and shake well to get rid of the water. Transfer the potato pieces to a bowl, sprinkle with the vinegar and leave to cool. Cover the bowl with plastic wrap and refrigerate for about 15 minutes.
3 Cut the ham into ¼-in (6-mm) squares. Slice the cucumber into thin rounds. Slice the onion thinly lengthwise. Place the cucumber and onion in a bowl and sprinkle with the ¼ teaspoon salt, then rub gently with your hands. When the vegetables turn limp, squeeze out any excess moisture.
4 Combine the potatoes and all the ingredients from step 3 in a large bowl. Add the mayonnaise, mix well, and then transfer to a serving plate.

Add the vinegar to the potatoes while they are still hot so that they absorb the flavor.

Rubbing the vegetables with salt helps them mix well with the mayonnaise.

Chinese-Style Mizuna Salad
with Sesame Dressing

Scallops and Daikon
with Sesame and Mayo

Izakaya Potato Salad

MACARONI SALAD with BLUE CHEESE and WALNUTS

The sharp umami of the blue cheese and the toasty flavor of the walnuts in this simple pasta salad are irresistible.

SERVES 2

2½ cups (625 ml) water
2 tablespoons shelled raw walnuts
3 oz (85 g) blue cheese, crumbled
1 tablespoon honey
1 teaspoon olive oil
Pinch of salt
½ cup (50 g) uncooked macaroni
Coarsely ground black pepper, to taste

1 Bring the water to a boil in a pan. Meanwhile, chop the walnuts coarsely so the pieces are about ½ in (1 cm) in size. Put about three-quarters of the blue cheese in a bowl and cream it with a wooden spoon. When the cheese is smooth, add the honey and mix it in. Add the olive oil, then the walnuts, mixing well with each addition.
2 When the water has come to a boil, add the salt and the macaroni. Cook following the directions on the package. When the macaroni is done, drain it well and add to the blue cheese mixture. Stir to combine and then leave to cool.
3 Transfer the macaroni salad to a serving plate. Crumble the remaining blue cheese on top and sprinkle the black pepper over all.

THAI-STYLE SALAD

This simple salad of bean sprouts, lettuce and carrots is given extra zing with a sweet-salty dressing.

SERVES 2

½ cup (55 g) fresh bean sprouts
¼ carrot
3 lettuce leaves
2 teaspoons coarsely chopped fresh cilantro (coriander leaves), or to taste
1 handful fresh mint leaves, or to taste
2 tablespoons roasted unsalted skinned peanuts, coarsely chopped

FOR THE DRESSING
1 teaspoon soy sauce
1 teaspoon fish sauce
1 teaspoon lime or lemon juice
1 teaspoon vegetable oil
¼ teaspoon sugar

1 Remove the roots and caps from the bean sprouts. Bring a generous amount of water to a boil in a pan, add the bean sprouts and blanch for about 30 seconds. Drain into a colander and leave to cool.
2 Peel the carrot and shred finely (see page 6). Stack the lettuce leaves together, roll up and shred (see How to Shred Cabbage on page 6). Arrange the vegetables, cilantro and mint leaves on a plate, scattering the peanuts over. Mix the dressing ingredients together and pour over the vegetables.

SHREDDED CABBAGE with SHIO KOMBU SEAWEED

Shio kombu is kombu seaweed that has been cooked until tender in soy sauce, sake and sugar. It's sold preserved in jars in Japanese groceries. The umami and saltiness of the shio kombu brings out the sweetness of the cabbage.

SERVES 2

2 small cabbage leaves
2 tablespoons shio kombu seaweed
1 tablespoon olive oil

Wash and dry the cabbage leaves, stack them together, roll up and shred them finely (see page 6). Combine the shredded cabbage in a bowl with the shio kombu and olive oil. Mix well and transfer to a serving bowl.

Macaroni Salad with
Blue Cheese and Walnuts

Thai-Style Salad

Shredded Cabbage with
Shio Kombu Seaweed

SPINACH NAMUL with SOY and SESAME

This Korean-style dish is flavored with sesame seeds and sesame oil.

SERVES 2

Pinch of salt
Bunch fresh spinach, washed, root
   ends removed
White sesame seeds, to taste

FOR THE SEASONING
1 teaspoon sesame oil
1 teaspoon soy sauce
Pinch of sea salt, to taste

1 Bring a generous amount of water to a boil in a pan with the pinch of salt. Add the spinach and blanch for about 1 minute. Drain and plunge into ice water to cool. Squeeze out the moisture and cut into 3-in (8-cm) pieces.
2 Combine the seasoning ingredients in a bowl and mix well. Add the spinach and mix. Arrange on a serving plate and sprinkle with the sesame seeds.

FRESHLY FRIED TORTILLA CHIPS

The fragrance of the cumin goes really well with these chips!

SERVES 2

1 soft flour tortilla, about 3 oz (85 g)
Oil for deep-frying
1/4 teaspoon sea salt, or to taste
1/4 teaspoon ground cumin, or to taste

1 Cut the tortilla into 1/2 x 2 in (1 x 5 cm) pieces.
2 Heat the oil to 355°F (180°C). Add the tortilla pieces and deep-fry for about 2 minutes, turning occasionally. Remove and drain on paper towels, then arrange on a serving plate and sprinkle with the salt and cumin.

SHRIMP and AVOCADO SPRING ROLLS

The red color of the shrimp and the green of the avocado, cilantro and mint leaves are a feast for the eyes as well as the taste buds. The garlic, miso and mayonnaise sauce is terrific too.

SERVES 2

2 shrimp, shells on
2 fresh rice-paper wrappers
1/4 avocado
2 loose-leaf lettuce leaves
Fresh cilantro (coriander leaves), to taste
Fresh mint leaves, to taste

FOR THE SAUCE
1/8 teaspoon minced garlic
1 1/2 tablespoons mayonnaise
1 teaspoon miso paste

1 Devein the shrimp. Bring a pan of water to boil, add the shrimp and blanch for about 90 seconds or until they turn red. Drain into a colander and allow to cool. Remove the shells and cut the shrimp in half lengthwise.
2 Cut the avocado into slices 1/2-in (1-cm) wide. Slice the lettuce leaves in half lengthwise. Chop the cilantro leaves coarsely. Tear up the mint leaves.
3 Pass the rice-paper wrappers quickly through a shallow bowl of water and lay them out on a kitchen towel that has been moistened and tightly wrung out.
4 Place a piece of the cut lettuce on the nearest edge of a spread-out rice wrapper. Top with a few cilantro leaves. Place some torn-up mint leaves on the far side of the wrapper and lay the shrimp and the avocado on top. Start rolling up the wrapper from the edge closest to you, folding in the left and right sides as you go. Keep the wrapper tight as you roll it around the filling, finishing with the edge of the wrapper under the roll. Repeat with the second wrapper.
5 Arrange the spring rolls on a serving plate. Mix the sauce ingredients together and serve alongside.

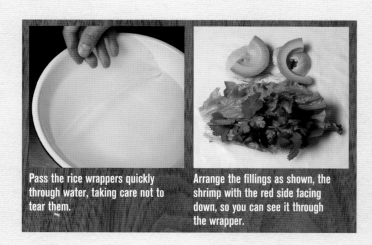

Pass the rice wrappers quickly through water, taking care not to tear them.

Arrange the fillings as shown, the shrimp with the red side facing down, so you can see it through the wrapper.

Spinach Namul with Soy and Sesame

Freshly Fried Tortilla Chips

Shrimp and Avocado Spring Rolls

TOMATO and EGG STIR-FRY

The acidity and sweetness of the tomato is the perfect foil for the soft and creamy eggs.

SERVES 2

1 small sweet tomato, or 4 large cherry tomatoes
1 tablespoon sesame oil
⅛ teaspoon minced fresh ginger
2 eggs, well beaten
Pinch of sea salt, to taste

1 Core the tomato and make a shallow crisscross cut into the skin at the bottom. Bring a pan of water to a boil and blanch the tomato for about 10 seconds, or until the skin starts to peel off. Transfer to ice water to cool, then peel carefully. Cut into 6 wedges.
2 Heat the sesame oil in a frying pan over medium heat. Add the tomato wedges and stir-fry for about 2 minutes. Add the minced ginger and stir.
3 Add the beaten eggs to the frying pan and cook, stirring constantly with a wooden spatula. When the eggs are softly set, stop stirring and let the bottom cook for 10 seconds. Immediately transfer to a serving plate and sprinkle with the salt.

KING OYSTER MUSHROOMS SAUTÉED in SOY BUTTER

These plump, delicious mushrooms are known as eringi in Japan. Portobello mushrooms also work well in this recipe.

SERVES 2

3 large king oyster mushrooms, or portobello mushrooms
¼ clove garlic
1 tablespoon olive oil
1 teaspoon unsalted butter
½ tablespoon soy sauce

1 Slice the mushrooms in half lengthwise and score the cut surfaces with a shallow crisscross pattern. Cut the scored mushroom pieces in half again crosswise. Slice the garlic into thin shreds.
2 Heat the olive oil in a frying pan over medium heat. Place the mushroom pieces in the pan, scored sides down. Cook for about 2 minutes, then turn them over and cook for an additional 2 minutes.
3 Put the butter in an empty part of the frying pan and add the garlic. Shake the pan to evenly distribute the contents and coat the mushrooms with the butter. Add the soy sauce, stir briefly, and serve.

BEAN SPROUTS and BACON

The crisp and crunchy texture of this dish makes it the perfect snack with drinks.

SERVES 2

5 oz (140 g) soybean or mung bean sprouts
2 slices bacon
½ teaspoon sea salt, or to taste
Soy sauce, to taste

1 Remove the roots and caps from the bean sprouts. Slice the bacon into strips ¼-in (6-mm) wide.
2 Place the bacon in a frying pan over low heat and stir-fry for about 3 minutes. When the fat begins to render out, turn the heat to high, add the bean sprouts and stir-fry for about 1 minute.
3 When everything in the pan is well coated with bacon fat, take the pan off the heat, add the salt and soy sauce and stir rapidly. Transfer to a serving plate.

PEA SHOOTS with FISH CAKE and SALTED WHITEBAIT

Dried salted whitebait—known as chirimenjako in Japanese—along with bonito flakes, add tons of umami to this dish.

SERVES 2

1 satsuma-age fish cake (see note, page 11), or Thai fish cake
4 oz (125 g) pea shoots
½ red Thai chili pepper, or to taste
½ tablespoon vegetable oil
2 tablespoons chirimenjako dried salted whitebait (see recipe headnote page 118)
Pinch of sea salt, to taste
Large pinch bonito flakes (see note, page 11)

1 Slice the fish cake into ¼-in (6-mm) strips. Cut the pea shoots in half. Remove the stem end and seeds from the chili pepper and slice into thin rounds.
2 Heat the oil in a frying pan over low heat. Add the chirimenjako and stir-fry for about 3 minutes. When the chirimenjako start to become crispy, add the fish cake and stir-fry for another minute.
3 When the ingredients in the pan are evenly coated with oil, raise the heat to medium, add the pea shoots and chili pepper, and stir-fry for another 3 minutes or so. When the pea shoots start to turn limp, add the salt and bonito flakes, stir quickly and transfer to a serving plate.

Tomato and Egg Stir-Fry

King Oyster Mushrooms
Sautéed in Soy Butter

Bean Sprouts and Bacon

Pea Shoots with Fish Cake and
Salted Whitebait

Fried Lotus Root

Spicy Konnyaku Kinpira Stir-Fry

FRIED LOTUS ROOT

Lotus root is the rhizome of the lotus flower plant. The holes running through it give the slices an attractive lacy appearance. You'll find it at Asian grocery stores.

SERVES 2

4-oz (125-g) piece lotus root, about ½ of a root (see note, above)
1 tablespoon olive oil
Pinch of sea salt, to taste
Dried red chili threads, to garnish (or substitute red pepper powder)

1 Cut the lotus root into slices ¼ in (6 mm) wide, put into a colander and rinse briefly under running water. Pat dry.
2 Heat the olive oil in a frying pan over low heat and add the lotus slices. Cook for about 10 minutes, then turn the slices over and cook for an additional 7 minutes or so. Season with the salt, transfer to a serving plate, and top with the red chili threads.

SPICY KONNYAKU KINPIRA STIR-FRY

A kinpira is a spicy stir-fry. This version is made with konnyaku, a gelatinous food made from starchy devil's-tongue root (a type of arrowroot) that is very healthy. Find konnyaku at a Japanese grocery; it comes in a block packed in a bag of water.

SERVES 2

1 block konnyaku, about 4 oz (125 g) (see note, above)
½ teaspoon sea salt

FOR THE SEASONING
½ red Thai chili pepper, deseeded and sliced into thin rounds
1 tablespoon soy sauce
½ tablespoon sugar
½ tablespoon mirin (see note, page 11)
1 teaspoon sesame oil

1 Combine all seasoning ingredients in a bowl and mix well.
2 Score both sides of the konnyaku in a crisscross pattern, then slice the block horizontally so that you end up with two thin slices. Cut each slice into strips ½ in (1 cm) wide. Sprinkle the strips with the ½ teaspoon salt and rub them with your hands. Place in a pan, add enough water to cover, and set over medium heat. Bring to a boil and cook for about a minute, then drain into a colander.
3 Put the konnyaku in a frying pan over low heat and stir-fry for about 3 minutes. When there is no moisture left in the pan, take it off the heat and add the seasoning mixture. Return to low heat and continue to cook, stirring constantly, until almost all moisture has evaporated. Transfer to a serving plate.

Chapter 2

GRILLED, ROASTED, BAKED, SAUTÉED

Grilled and roasted chicken, grilled fish, pan-fried gyoza dumplings—these are all essential elements of any izakaya menu. The crisp textures and wonderful aromas of the izakaya foods in this category always make my heart dance with joy. Even though some recipes here may be a challenge at first, as you make the same things two or three times and more, you'll master them and they'll become your own. Always aim for that perfectly browned, crispy finish.

CHICKEN SKEWERS and ROAST CHICKEN

I have included recipes for standard izakaya yakitori chicken skewers like *negima* (grilled skewers of chicken and leek) and *tsukune* (chicken meatballs on skewers with a sweet-salty sauce), as well as dishes with the flavors of South and Southeast Asia such as Chicken Satay Skewers, Pan-Fried Cilantro Chicken and Oven-Roasted Tandoori Chicken. Enjoy the process as you make each delicious dish.

CHICKEN and LEEK SKEWERS

Called *negima* in Japanese, these tasty skewers are seasoned simply with salt so that the flavor of the chicken really comes through. The skewers are browned to perfection in a frying pan.

2 SKEWERS

1 boneless chicken thigh meat, skin on
6-in (16-cm) length Japanese or baby leek, or
    thick green onion, roots trimmed
2 bamboo skewers
Sea salt, for sprinkling, to taste
½ tablespoon vegetable oil

1 Cut the chicken into 6 bite-sized pieces. Discard the green part of the leek, trim the white part and cut into quarters. Thread pieces of chicken and leek in alternating order onto 2 skewers and sprinkle with salt.
2 Heat the vegetable oil in a frying pan over medium heat. Place the skewers in the pan skin side down. Cook for about 3 minutes. Turn the skewers over, cook for an additional 3 minutes, and arrange on a serving plate.

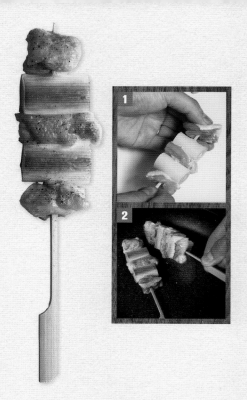

SWEET and SOUR CHICKEN MEATBALL SKEWERS

Crunchy-textured cartilage is a tasty surprise in these chicken meatballs, called *tsukune* in Japan. For an authentic Japanese touch, dip into egg yolk before eating!

2 SKEWERS

1 oz (30 g) chicken cartilage pieces
2-in (5-cm) length Japanese or
    baby leek, or thick green onion
    (white part only)
2 green onions (scallions)
4 oz (125 g) ground chicken
2 wide bamboo skewers
1 tablespoon vegetable oil
2 raw egg yolks (optional)

FOR THE SEASONING
1 teaspoon minced fresh ginger
1 teaspoon sake
1 teaspoon mirin (see note,
    page 11)
Pinch of sea salt, to taste
Pinch of black pepper

FOR THE SAUCE
½ teaspoon sake
½ teaspoon mirin (see note,
    page 11)
½ teaspoon soy sauce
1 teaspoon sugar

1 Finely chop the cartilage and leek. Discard the white part of the green onions and slice the greens into thin rounds. Combine the ground chicken, cartilage, leek, and green onions in a bowl, add the seasoning ingredients and mix well with your hands.
2 Divide the meat mixture into 2 equal portions. Put each portion on a wide skewer, using your hands to mold it around the skewer evenly and smoothly.
3 Heat the oil in a frying pan over medium-low heat. Place the skewers in the pan and cook for about 6 minutes. Turn over and cook for 4 more minutes. When both sides are browned, mix the sauce ingredients together and add to the frying pan. Simmer while shaking the pan to coat the meatballs with the sauce. Serve on individual plates with the egg yolks on the side.

Mix using a squeezing motion until the meat mixture is sticky.

CHICKEN SATAY SKEWERS

It's easy to recreate Southeast Asian flavors at home using peanut butter and Thai fish sauce to make the satay.

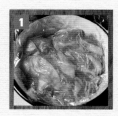

4 SKEWERS

1 boneless chicken thigh, skin on
4 bamboo skewers, soaked in water
½ tablespoon vegetable oil

FOR THE MARINADE

¼ teaspoon minced garlic
1 tablespoon soy sauce
1 tablespoon honey
1 tablespoon unsweetened peanut butter
1 teaspoon fish sauce
Red pepper powder, to taste

1 Combine the marinade ingredients in a small bowl and mix well. Cut the chicken into 16 bite-sized pieces and place in a larger bowl. Pour the marinade ingredients over the chicken and mix well with your hands until the meat is well coated. Put a sheet of plastic wrap directly on top of the chicken inside the bowl and refrigerate for 30 minutes or more.
2 Thread an equal number of chicken pieces onto each skewer with the skin side down.
3 Heat the vegetable oil in a frying pan over medium heat. Place the skewers in the pan with the skin side down and cook for about 3 minutes. Turn and cook for another 3 minutes, and arrange on a serving plate.

PAN-FRIED CILANTRO CHICKEN

These chicken drumettes are sprinkled with lots of chopped cilantro; the lime juice adds a tangy flavor.

6 PIECES

6 chicken drumettes (the thickest section of a chicken wing)
1 tablespoon vegetable oil

FOR THE MARINADE

½ cup (30 g) chopped fresh cilantro (coriander leaves)
¼ teaspoon minced garlic
1 tablespoon fish sauce
2 teaspoons freshly squeezed lime or lemon juice
Large pinch of sea salt, or to taste

1 Combine the marinade ingredients in a bowl and mix well.
2 Put the chicken drumettes and the marinade into a resealable plastic bag. Close the bag and shake and squeeze it around. Refrigerate overnight.
3 Remove the chicken from the bag, reserving the marinade, and lightly pat dry with paper towels. Heat the vegetable oil in a frying pan over medium heat, add the chicken pieces, and pan-fry, stirring, for about 10 minutes. When the chicken is browned all over, add the remaining marinade from the plastic bag. Heat until it bubbles, shaking the pan to coat the chicken, and then transfer to a serving plate.

OVEN-ROASTED TANDOORI CHICKEN

Use whole chicken legs to make an impact. Roast them in the oven so they cook up plump and juicy.

2 CHICKEN LEGS

2 chicken legs
½ teaspoon minced garlic
½ teaspoon minced fresh ginger
½ cup (110 g) plain yogurt
2 teaspoons curry powder
2 teaspoons sea salt, or to taste
½ teaspoon lemon juice

1 Make cuts halfway into the chicken leg along the bones. Make a cut into the joint as well. Combine all the other ingredients in a large bowl and mix well. Add the chicken leg to the bowl and coat with the marinade. Place the chicken on a plate, and cover directly with plastic wrap. Refrigerate overnight.
2 Preheat the oven to 400°F (200°C). Line a baking sheet with parchment paper. Remove the plastic wrap from the marinated chicken leg and place on the baking sheet, skin side up. Roast for 30 minutes until golden brown. Serve.

JAPANESE ROAST PORK

Japanese-style roast pork is similar to Cantonese-style roast pork (char siu).
Use a shoulder cut so that you can enjoy both the lean meat and the fat of the pork.

SERVES 4-6

1 lb (500 g) pork shoulder
1 Japanese or baby leek, or thick
   green onion

FOR THE MARINADE

1 teaspoon minced garlic
1 teaspoon minced fresh ginger
3 tablespoons soy sauce
2 tablespoons honey
1 tablespoon sake
1 tablespoon tianmianjiang sweet
   bean sauce*
1 teaspoon sesame oil
1 teaspoon ground Sichuan pepper
1 star anise pod, or ½ teaspoon
   five-spice powder

*Tianmianjiang is a sweet-and-savory fermented wheat and soybean paste from Sichuan province in China. It can be found in Chinese grocery stores and some Japanese grocery stores–in the latter, it's called *teimenjan*.

1 Combine the marinade ingredients in a bowl and mix well. Put the pork and the marinade in a resealable plastic bag. Seal the bag and shake around to coat the meat well. Refrigerate overnight.

2 Preheat the oven to 355°F (180°C). Line a baking tray with kitchen parchment paper and place a roasting rack on it. Remove the pork from the bag, reserving the marinade, place on the rack and roast for about 40 minutes. As it roasts, use a brush to baste it three or four times with the reserved marinade. Save some marinade to make the sauce later.

3 Poke the middle part of the roast with a skewer; if the juices run clear, the meat is done. If the juices are still pink, roast for a few more minutes. When the meat is done, take it out of the oven and set aside to rest.

4 Discard the green part of the leek. Trim and thinly slice the white part on the diagonal and soak in a bowl

Letting the sliced leeks stand in cold water for a few minutes removes their bite.

of cold water for about 3 minutes. Drain.

5 Pass the reserved marinade through a sieve or tea strainer into a small pan. Simmer over low heat while stirring with a wooden spatula for about 5 minutes or until thick. Slice the pork, arrange on a serving plate, pour the sauce over it and top with the sliced leeks.

GRILLED WAGYU STEAK JAPANESE STYLE

Reward yourself once in a while with a nice steak! Here I've used a fillet, which is not too fatty, cooked at just the right temperature, served with lots of grated daikon radish and green shiso leaves. If you want to really splurge, use finely marbled wagyu—premium Japan-raised beef.

SERVES 2-4

4-in (10-cm) length daikon radish (see note, page 11)
6 green shiso leaves (see note, page 12)
1 lb (500 g) well-marbled beef fillet
½ teaspoon sea salt, or to taste
Coarsely ground black pepper, to taste
4 tablespoons vegetable oil

FOR THE SAUCE
1 tablespoon soy sauce
1 tablespoon sake
1½ teaspoons mirin (see note, page 11)

1 Peel and grate the daikon radish, then place it in a fine-mesh colander or sieve to drain off excess moisture.
2 Remove the stems from the shiso leaves, halve the leaves lengthwise and cut crosswise into ¼-in (6-mm) wide strips.
3 Combine the sauce ingredients in a small microwave-safe bowl. Cover the bowl loosely with plastic wrap and microwave for about 30 seconds.
4 Just before cooking, season the steak on both sides with the salt and black pepper.
5 Heat the oil in a frying pan over high heat. Add the seasoned steak and sear for about a minute. Turn and sear for another minute. Transfer to a rack set over a baking tray and leave to rest for about a minute. Slice the steak into ¾-in (2-cm) squares and arrange on a serving plate with the grated daikon radish. Pour the sauce over and scatter the shiso leaves on top.

PORK STEAK with APPLE GINGER SAUCE and FRIED GARLIC

This pork steak is browned to a nice turn in garlic-infused oil. Serve it with a delicious sauce flavored with apple.

SERVES 2

1 clove garlic
1 1/2 tablespoons olive oil, divided
2 slices onion, 1/4 in (6 mm) thick
8 oz (225 g) pork shoulder steak
1/4 teaspoon sea salt, or to taste
Coarsely ground black pepper, to taste
1 teaspoon unsalted butter
1 tablespoon French-style mustard

FOR THE SAUCE
1/4 apple, grated
1/2 teaspoon minced fresh ginger
1 tablespoon sake
1 tablespoon soy sauce
1 tablespoon mirin (see note, page 11)

1 Combine the sauce ingredients in a bowl and mix. Cut the garlic clove in half.
2 Heat 1/2 tablespoon of the olive oil in a frying pan over medium heat. Add the onions and fry for about 3 minutes. Turn over and fry for another 3 minutes. Transfer to a serving plate.
3 Season both sides of the pork with the salt and black pepper. Heat the remaining 1 tablespoon of olive oil and the garlic in the frying pan over low heat. Gently fry the garlic for about 3 minutes, turning occasionally.
4 When the garlic has lightly browned, put the seasoned pork in the frying pan and fry for about 3 minutes. Turn and cook for another 3 minutes. Remove and reserve the garlic.
5 Add the butter to the pan, then add the sauce ingredients. Cook until the sauce coats the meat and is reduced. Remove the pork, slice it and arrange on top of the onions from step 2. Pour the sauce from the frying pan over the pork. Put the reserved garlic and the mustard in a small bowl alongside, and dip the pork pieces in the mustard-garlic as you eat.

When the garlic is lightly browned and fragrant, put the seasoned pork in the frying pan and fry for about 3 minutes.

CHICKEN TERIYAKI with CRUNCHY GREENS

Give the chicken a beautiful sheen and flavor with this sweet-salty sauce. If you can't find komatsuna greens at your farmers' market or Asian grocery store, use fresh spinach or bok choy instead.

SERVES 2

1 bunch komatsuna, spinach or
   bok choy, about 10 oz (300 g)
Pinch of salt
1 tablespoon water
2 boneless chicken thighs,
   skin on
½ tablespoon vegetable oil

FOR THE SAUCE

4 tablespoons soy sauce
2 tablespoons sake
2 tablespoons mirin (see note,
   page 11)
1 teaspoon sugar

1 Wash and trim the greens. Spread them out in a frying pan, add the salt and water, cover with a lid and place over medium heat. When the water comes to a boil, steam, still covered, for 1 minute. Drain into a colander. Combine the sauce ingredients in a bowl and mix well.

2 Make several shallow incisions with a sharp knife in the chicken thighs to sever the muscle fibers in the meat on the side without skin (see Oven-Roasted Tandoori Chicken, page 41). This prevents the chicken from shrinking when fried. In a clean pan heat the vegetable oil over medium-low heat. Put the chicken thighs in the pan, skin side down, and fry for 5 minutes, pushing down on the meat occasionally with a wooden spatula. Turn and cook the meat on the other side for 3 more minutes, blotting up excess fat from the frying pan with paper towel as you go.

3 Reduce heat to low, add the sauce to the pan, cover the pan with a lid and cook for about 3 minutes. Occasionally turn the chicken to coat with the sauce. When there is very little moisture left in the pan, take the chicken out and slice into easy-to-eat pieces.

4 Line a serving plate with the cooked komatsuna greens and arrange the chicken on top. Pour the remaining sauce from the frying pan on top.

Turn the chicken while cooking to coat in the sauce.

PAN-FRIED SEA BREAM with SAKE-BRAISED CLAMS and BROCCOLINI

In Japan this recipe is made using nanohana, the flower stalks of a plant closely related to broccoli and rapeseed. You may be able to find it at Japanese grocery stores or farmer's markets. If not, broccoli rabe or broccolini make good substitutes.

SERVES 2

8 asari clams or little neck clams in their shells, well cleaned and rinsed under running water (see note, page 108)
4–5 stalks broccoli rabe or broccolini, cut into bite-sized pieces
½ clove garlic, chopped finely
2 sea bream fillets, about 12 oz (350 g) total
½ teaspoon sea salt, or to taste
Coarsely ground black pepper, to taste
1 tablespoon flour
3 tablespoons olive oil, divided
½ red Thai chili pepper, or to taste
1 tablespoon sake
Scant ½ cup (100 ml) water
2 slices lemon
1 teaspoon soy sauce

1 Pat the sea bream fillets dry with paper towels. Season both sides with salt and pepper and dust with the flour.
2 Heat 1 tablespoon of the olive oil in a frying pan over medium heat. Put in the sea bream fillets skin-side down and pan-fry for about 3 minutes.
3 When the skin side of the sea bream has browned, turn the pieces over and cook for another minute or so. When both sides are browned, transfer the sea bream to a serving plate.
4 Heat another 1 tablespoon of the olive oil in the frying pan over medium heat, along with the garlic and chili pepper.
5 When the garlic starts to smell fragrant, add the clams and broccoli rabe and stir-fry quickly.
6 Sprinkle the sake over the clams and broccoli rabe, stir briefly and add the water. Cover with a lid and steam-fry for about a minute. When the clams have opened, remove the lid and add the lemon slices and soy sauce and the remaining tablespoon of olive oil. Shake the frying pan around to distribute seasonings evenly, then pour the contents over the sea bream.

SPICY STUFFED SARDINES AU GRATIN

Stuff the sardines with mentaiko (spiced salted fish roe), coat with creamy béchamel sauce and bake.

Mentaiko roe, a traditional Japanese ingredient, gets a Western twist.

SERVES 2

2 large whole fresh sardines
½ teaspoon sea salt, divided
1½ tablespoons unsalted butter
2 tablespoons flour
1 scant cup (200 ml) whole milk
2 tablespoons mentaiko roe (see note, page 11)
1 cup (125 g) shredded pizza cheese

1 Open up the sardines from the belly side (see page 10) with the heads still on and sprinkle with ¼ teaspoon of the salt. Place on a shallow tray, cover with plastic wrap and refrigerate for about an hour. Pat dry with paper towels. Preheat the oven to 430°F (220°C).

2 Make the béchamel sauce: Melt the butter in a frying pan over medium heat, add the flour and stir. When the flour has absorbed the butter and no longer looks floury, add the milk a little at a time, stirring constantly. When the sauce has thickened, add the remaining ¼ teaspoon salt, stir well and take the pan off the heat.

3 Cut into the membrane surrounding the mentaiko sac and scrape out the eggs. Spread the mentaiko on the inner side of the sardines and place them on an ovenproof baking dish. Pour the béchamel sauce over the sardines, sprinkle the cheese on top, and bake in the oven for about 15 minutes.

Spread the mentaiko roe on the inner side of the sardines.

ROASTED SARDINES with ORANGE SAUCE

A sweet-and-sour sauce of pine nuts, raisins and orange enhances the distinctive umami of the sardines.

SERVES 2

2 large whole fresh sardines
½ orange
1 tablespoon raisins, or sultanas
1 tablespoon pine nuts
Pinch of sea salt
1 tablespoon olive oil

FOR THE BREADCRUMBS
Grated peel of half an orange*
2 tablespoons panko breadcrumbs
¼ teaspoon sea salt, or to taste

*Before grating the orange, rub the surface with a pinch of salt, rinse well with water and pat dry.

1 Preheat the oven to 430°F (220°C). Open up the sardines with your hands (see page 10) and salt both sides. Roll up each sardine from the head end and secure with a wooden toothpick. Segment the orange (see page 7) and cut the segments in half.

2 Combine the breadcrumb ingredients in a bowl and mix. Line a baking tray with kitchen parchment paper, put the sardines on it and top with the breadcrumbs. Roast in the oven for about 15 minutes, until browned.

3 Meanwhile, heat the olive oil in a frying pan over low heat. Add the pine nuts and stir-fry until fragrant. Turn the heat to medium, add the orange segments and raisins and stir-fry briefly. Transfer the sauce to a serving plate. Remove the toothpicks from the sardines and arrange on top of the sauce.

Open up the sardines with your hands.

SPANISH MACKEREL with SALTED PLUM MISO SAUCE

This delicious sauce works well with other fish too. Try cod, amberjack, yellowtail, salmon or swordfish.

SERVES 2

2 Spanish mackerel fillets, about 10 oz (300 g) total
2 small umeboshi pickled plums, soft type (see note, page 12)
3 green shiso leaves (see note, page 12)

FOR THE SEASONING
2 teaspoons white miso paste
2 teaspoons sake
2 teaspoons mirin (see note, page 11)

1 Pat the fish dry with paper towels and cut in half lengthwise. Pit the umeboshi and chop to make a paste. Remove the stems from the shiso leaves and chop finely.
2 Combine the umeboshi paste, the shiso and the seasoning ingredients in a small bowl and mix well.
3 Place the fish on a baking sheet and spread the ume-miso sauce on top. Bake in the oven preheated to about 400°F (200°C) for around 15 minutes. Transfer to individual serving plates.

Pit the umeboshi and chop to make a paste.

MISO CURED BAKED COD

If you can find tender young Japanese turnips, they work well in this dish. Sake, served hot or bracingly chilled, goes very well with the fragrant miso.

SERVES 2

2 fresh cod fillets, about 10 oz (300 g)
¼ teaspoon sea salt
2 baby turnips, about 4 oz (125 g)

FOR THE MISO MARINADE
⅓ cup (100 g) miso paste*
2 teaspoons mirin (see note, page 11)
2 teaspoons sake
1 teaspoon sugar

*Use miso that has a salt content of about 5% for this recipe. Saikyo miso or a mild white miso are good choices.

1 Salt the cod pieces, place in a shallow tray, cover with plastic wrap and refrigerate for about an hour. Pat dry with paper towels.
2 Combine the miso marinade ingredients in a bowl. Wrap the cod with cheesecloth, spread the miso marinade over all, cover with plastic wrap and refrigerate overnight.
3 Peel the turnips, leaving about ½ in (1 cm) of the stems. Halve the turnips crosswise about ½ in (1 cm) from the top. Blanch in boiling water for about a minute, then drain.
4 Cut a piece of aluminum foil about 8-in (20-cm) long. Crumple it up, then spread it out again and place it on a baking tray. Un-wrap the cod and place it on the foil. Spread a little of the miso marinade on the turnip pieces and place on the foil. Bake in the oven preheated to 400°F (200°C) for around 10 minutes. Remove the turnips and bake the cod for an additional 5 minutes. Arrange the cod and turnips on a serving plate.

Wrap the cod with cheesecloth and spread the marinade over all.

SQUID STEAKS WITH TOMATOES and CAPERS

Use the sweet, juicy sautéed tomatoes as a sauce for the squid. Tangy capers really enhance this dish.

SERVES 2

8 oz (225 g) fresh or frozen squid, body only (guts, legs, skin and cartilage removed)*
5 cherry tomatoes
2 teaspoons capers
½ teaspoon sea salt, or to taste
Black pepper, to taste
1 tablespoon olive oil
2 teaspoons butter
2 teaspoons lemon juice
2 teaspoons soy sauce
1 sprig flat-leaf parsley

*Choose a fresh or frozen squid with a thick body. See page 8 for how to clean and prepare squid.

1 Score the surface of the squid in a shallow crisscross pattern, then cut into 1 x 2 in (2.5 x 5 cm) pieces. Stem the cherry tomatoes and cut in half lengthwise. Drain the capers. Season the squid with the salt and pepper.
2 Heat the olive oil in a frying pan over medium heat. Add the squid with the scored sides facing down and sauté for about 2 minutes. Turn the squid, add the cherry tomatoes and the butter, and cook for another minute or so.
3 When the squid has browned, take the pan off the heat and add the drained capers, lemon juice, soy sauce and parsley. Shake the frying pan around to coat the squid with the flavors. Transfer to a serving plate and scatter parsley leaves on top.

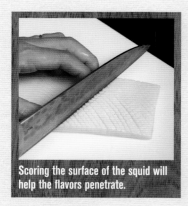

Scoring the surface of the squid will help the flavors penetrate.

STIR-FRIED SHRIMP with SAKE, GARLIC and FISH SAUCE

The key to cooking shrimp in their shells properly is to do it over high heat so that they turn crispy and fragrant. The sake, garlic and fish sauce add lots of flavor.

SERVES 2

6 jumbo shrimp in their shells
1 clove garlic
1½ tablespoons vegetable oil
1 tablespoon sake
2 tablespoons fish sauce
1 teaspoon soy sauce

1 Cut into the shrimp down the backs and devein. Mince the garlic finely (see page 7).

2 Heat the vegetable oil in a frying pan over high heat. Add the shrimp and pan-fry for about a minute. Turn over and cook for another minute or so. When the shrimp is brown and crisp, add the garlic.

3 When the garlic is lightly browned, sprinkle in the sake, take the pan off the heat and add the fish sauce and soy sauce. Shake the frying pan around to coat the shrimp with the flavors. Transfer to a serving plate.

Cut into the shrimp about halfway while turning your knife to open up the back.

BAKED TOFU NAMERO

Namero is a classic izakaya dish that's usually made with raw chopped fish. Here I have used tofu for a healthy alternative.

SERVES 2

1 block firm silken tofu, about 12 oz (350 g)
2 myoga ginger buds (see note, page 11)
3 green onions (scallions)
1 egg yolk
3 teaspoons minced fresh ginger
3 tablespoons miso paste
2 teaspoons soy sauce

1 Wrap the tofu in a piece of un-bleached cheesecloth or muslin. Place the wrapped tofu under a flat plate or tray. Put about 1 cup (250 ml) water in a bowl and place it on the tray as a weight. Leave for an hour to drain.

2 Finely chop the myoga ginger. Discard the whites of the green onions and slice the greens into thin rounds.

3 Put the drained tofu and all the other ingredients on a cutting board. Mix well while chopping everything finely with a kitchen knife to make a paste.

4 Spread the paste on a 8 x 8 in (20 x 20 cm) baking sheet lined with aluminum foil. Bake in the oven preheated to 400°F (200°C) for about 10 minutes. Serve hot.

SEASONED JAPANESE OMELETTE

The dashi stock in this omelette makes it melt-in-your-mouth tender. Grated daikon radish with soy sauce is the perfect accompaniment on top.

SERVES 2

Generous pinch dried hijiki seaweed*

2-in (5-cm) length daikon radish (see note, page 11)

4 eggs

1 tablespoon vegetable oil

½ teaspoon soy sauce

½ cup (125 ml) water

1 tablespoon soy sauce

1 tablespoon mirin (see note, page 11)

FOR THE SEASONING

2½ tablespoons dashi stock (see page 6)

1 tablespoon sugar

½ teaspoon sea salt, or to taste

1 Rinse the hijiki under running water and soak in enough water to cover for about 20 minutes to reconstitute. Drain and put into a pan with the water, soy sauce and mirin, then turn the heat to medium. When the liquid comes to a boil, remove from heat and leave the pan to cool as-is for about 20 minutes. Drain the hijiki in a colander and cut into ½-in (1-cm) pieces (if the hijiki is not pre-cut).

2 Peel the daikon radish, grate and leave to drain in a fine-meshed sieve.

3 Break the eggs into a bowl. Add the seasoning ingredients and beat well. Add the drained hijiki and mix briefly.

4 Heat the vegetable oil in a small frying pan over medium heat. Pour in the egg mixture. Mix the egg around in the pan with a fork for about 30 seconds or until the egg is softly set. Turn the heat down to low, cover the pan with a lid and steam-cook for about 3 minutes.

5 Turn the omelette pan over onto a flat lid or board and slide the omelette onto a plate. Top with the grated daikon radish and drizzle with the soy sauce.

*Hijiki is a brown seaweed with short, thin leaves. It's available as *me-hijiki* (hijiki shoots), and *kuki-hijiki* or *naga-hijiki*, which are longer and thicker. Me-hijiki is easier to find and doesn't need cutting up for most dishes. Almost all hijiki sold outside Japan is dried, and needs to be reconstituted before using. When soaked in water it increases to about eight times its original volume.

Mix in the melted cheese and enjoy!

BAKED POTATOES GRATIN with FISH ROE

These cheesy, salty baked potatoes are made with tarako salted cod or pollack roe. You'll find it in Japanese grocery stores, where it is usually sold frozen. Defrost tarako in the fridge and eat on the day it is defrosted. You can also use salmon roe, caviar or tobiko roe.

SERVES 2

2 potatoes, skins on
1 tablespoon tarako roe (see note, above) or salmon roe
2 teaspoons butter
½ teaspoon sea salt, or to taste
¼ cup (30 g) shredded pizza cheese

1 Wash the potatoes and remove the eyes. Place them in a microwave-safe dish, cover loosely with plastic wrap and microwave for 16–20 minutes. They are done when a skewer goes through them easily.

2 Cut the tops off the cooked potatoes. Holding onto them with a dry kitchen towel so you don't burn yourself, scoop out the flesh into a bowl. Add the tarako, butter and salt to the scooped-out potato and stir well.

3 Stuff each of the potato shells from step 2 half full with the mixture from step 2. Stuff half of the cheese into the shells, then add the remaining potato mixture. Top with the rest of the cheese.

4 Line a baking sheet with aluminum foil and put the stuffed potatoes on it. Bake in the oven preheated to 400°F (200°C) for about 5 minutes, or until the tops are browned.

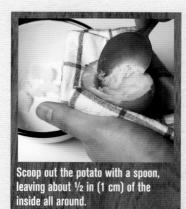

Scoop out the potato with a spoon, leaving about ½ in (1 cm) of the inside all around.

STUFFED SAUTÉED SHIITAKE MUSHROOMS

These juicy morsels are packed with the umami of the ground pork, ginger, and sake.

SERVES 2

4-in (10-cm) length Japanese or
  baby leek, or thick green onion,
  (white part only) trimmed and
  chopped
4 large fresh shiitake mushrooms
6 oz (170 g) ground pork
Sea salt for sprinkling, to taste
Flour for sprinkling
1 tablespoon vegetable oil
⅓ teaspoon minced fresh ginger

FOR THE SEASONING

1 teaspoon sake
1 teaspoon soy sauce
1 teaspoon cornstarch
Pinch of sea salt, to taste

1 Make several cuts along the length of the leek, then chop finely. Cut the stems off the shiitake mushrooms, discarding the hard ends. Finely chop the rest of the stems.

2 Combine the ground pork, the chopped leek, the chopped shiitake stems, and the seasoning ingredients in a bowl and mix well. Divide into four equal portions.

3 Sprinkle a little salt and flour on the insides of the mushroom caps. Stuff with the meat mixture, forming an even mound in each cap.

4 Heat the vegetable oil in a frying pan over low heat. Add the stuffed mushroom caps, meat side down, and cook for about 2 minutes. When the meat is browned, turn the mushroom caps over, cover with a lid and cook for another 5 minutes or so. Transfer to a serving plate and top each with a dab of minced ginger.

If you dust the insides of the mushrooms caps with flour, the filling will be less likely to fall out. Form the filling into a nice rounded shape.

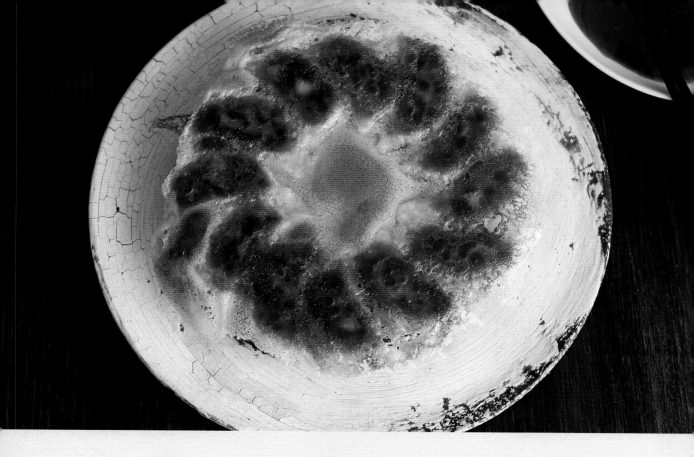

CRISPY FRIED GYOZA DUMPLINGS

These dumplings have crispy "wings" and a nutty sesame flavor. Find fresh or frozen wrappers for dumplings (gyoza in Japanese, wontons in Chinese) at Asian markets or general supermarkets.

SERVES 2

3 large cabbage leaves
¼ teaspoon sea salt
Small bunch chives, about 1 oz (30 g)
4-in (10-cm) length Japanese or baby leek, or thick green onion (white part only) trimmed
4 oz (125 g) ground pork
12 round dumpling wrappers
1 teaspoon flour
2½ tablespoons water
½ tablespoon sesame oil

FOR THE SEASONING

½ teaspoon minced garlic
½ teaspoon minced fresh ginger
1 tablespoon sake
½ teaspoon sesame oil
¼ teaspoon sea salt, or to taste
Black pepper, to taste

1 Chop the cabbage finely and place into a bowl. Sprinkle with the salt and massage by hand. When the cabbage turns limp, squeeze it tightly to remove excess moisture.

2 Chop the chives finely. Make several cuts along the length of the leek and chop finely.

3 Combine the pork, cabbage, chives and leek into a bowl along with the seasoning ingredients and mix well. Divide the mixture into 12 equal portions. Put one portion onto a gyoza skin and brush the edge of the skin lightly with water. Fold the skin in half, pinch in the middle, and pleat the skin 2 to 3 times toward the middle to wrap the filling and form the dumpling. Repeat with the remaining filling and skins.

4 Place a nonstick frying pan over medium heat. Arrange the gyoza dumplings in a ring and cook for about 3 minutes. When the bottoms of the dumplings have started to brown lightly, mix the flour and water together and add to the pan. Raise the heat to high, cover the pan with a lid and steam-fry for another 3 minutes.

5 When there is almost no moisture left in the pan, remove the lid, lower the heat to medium, and pour in the sesame oil from the sides of the pan. Cook for another 3 minutes. Invert a plate onto the frying pan, flip it over to transfer the dumplings onto the plate, and serve.

The slippery-smooth texture of these boiled dumplings is irresistible

SIMMERED CHICKEN GYOZA

Shiso leaves, salted plums and bamboo shoots add a delicious flavor and fragrance to these delicious chicken gyoza dumplings.

SERVES 2

- 1 umeboshi salted plum, soft type (see note, page 12)
- 1½ oz (40 g) ready-cooked bamboo shoot*
- 2 green shiso leaves (see note, page 12)
- 4 oz (125 g) ground chicken
- ½ tablespoon sake
- ½ tablespoon soy sauce
- 12 round dumpling wrappers
- ½ tablespoon sesame oil
- 2 green onions (scallions), green parts only, thinly sliced

*Bamboo Shoots Young bamboo shoots are eaten as a vegetable throughout East Asia. Cooked bamboo shoots, vacuum packed or canned, are available at Asian markets. The vacuum-packed ones are in the refrigerated section.

1 Remove the pit from the umeboshi and chop into a paste. Chop the bamboo shoot finely. Discard the stems from the shiso and chop the leaves finely.

2 Combine the ground chicken, umeboshi, bamboo shoot, shiso, sake and soy sauce in a bowl and mix well. Divide the mixture into 12 equal portions. Put one portion of the mixture onto a gyoza skin and brush the edge of the skin lightly with water. Fold the skin in half, pinch in the middle, and pleat the skin 4 to 5 times toward the middle to wrap the filling and form the dumpling. (Note: that these dumplings have more folds than the pan-fried ones opposite, giving them a frillier appearance.) Repeat with the remaining filling and skins.

3 Bring a generous amount of water to a boil in a pan, then add the dumplings. When they float to the surface of the water, scoop them out with a slotted spoon, drain briefly, and arrange on a serving plate. Sprinkle with the sesame oil and green onions and serve.

When the gyoza float to the top and the skins look translucent, they're done.

OKONOMIYAKI STUFFED JAPANESE PANCAKE

This savory pancake uses yamatoimo (Japanese mountain yam), a relative of the Chinese yam with a much thicker, stickier texture; this makes the pancakes fluffy and tender. Chinese yam can be used instead (see note in step 2). Aonori powder, made from nori seaweed, is a tasty final touch.

SERVES 2

6 oz (170 g) yamatoimo (see note, above) or Chinese yam (see note, page 11)
Small bunch enoki mushrooms, about 2 oz (60 g)
1 large fresh shiitake mushroom
1 small cabbage leaf
2 green onions (scallions)
1/4 teaspoon sea salt, or to taste
2 to 3 tablespoons cornstarch (if using Chinese yam)
1/2 tablespoon vegetable oil
3 tablespoons okonomiyaki sauce (see note, page 78)
2 teaspoons mayonnaise
Aonori powder,* to taste
Bonito flakes (see note, page 11), to garnish

1 Peel and grate the yam. Cut the roots from the enoki mushrooms, then halve them crosswise. Remove the stem from the shiitake mushroom, discarding the hard end, and chop finely. Slice the shiitake cap thinly. Shred the cabbage. Trim the green onions and slice both white and green parts into 1-in (3-cm) lengths.

2 Combine all the ingredients from step 1 in a large bowl. Add the salt and mix to a smooth batter with a wooden spoon. (Note: If you are using Chinese yam, add 2 to 3 tablespoons of cornstarch until the batter is quite thick. Mix well until the cornstarch is incorporated.)

Mix well so the grated yam coats the other ingredients thoroughly.

3 Heat the vegetable oil in a small frying pan over medium-high heat. Add the batter, cover with a lid and cook for about 5 minutes. Turn the pancake and cook for an additional 3 minutes or so. Turn over again, transfer to a plate, and drizzle the okonomiyaki sauce and mayonnaise over. Scatter the aonori powder and bonito flakes on top.

*****Aonori** is dried, powdered nori seaweed. It's used as a garnish on noodles, okonomiyaki savory pancake and more. Find aonori at Japanese grocery stores and online. Store opened packets in a cool, dry place.

Chapter 3

DEEP-FRIED

Crispy Fried Chicken Nuggets, Taro and Potato Croquettes, Tofu Fritters with Edamame . . . these izakaya favorites are easy to make at home. Biting into a crisp, piping-hot, freshly deep-fried morsel while slowly enjoying an ice-cold beer or highball is a great way to unwind.

CRISPY FRIED CHICKEN NUGGETS

Sometimes I just crave freshly cooked chicken karaage—Japanese-style fried chicken nuggets—which are crunchy on the outside, plump and juicy on the inside. Here I show you how to make the standard karaage that everyone loves, plus a variation using a marmalade glaze that is scrumptious!

SERVES 2-4

2 boneless chicken thighs, skin on
2½ tablespoons flour
Oil for deep-frying
2 large cabbage leaves, finely
    shredded (see page 6)

FOR THE MARINADE
2 tablespoons minced garlic
2 tablespoons minced fresh ginger
6 tablespoons sake
6 tablespoons soy sauce
Black pepper, to taste

1 Cut the chicken thighs into bite-sized pieces and put into a bowl. Add the marinade ingredients and rub them into the chicken with your hands. Cover the bowl with plastic wrap and refrigerate for 30 minutes to an hour.
2 Remove the chicken from the fridge and take off the wrap. Sprinkle the flour over and mix to coat the chicken.
3 Heat the oil to 355°F (180°C). Add the coated chicken pieces one at a time and fry for about 90 seconds.
4 When the chicken is lightly browned all over, take it out and let rest for about 4 minutes on a paper-towel-lined plate to drain the oil. The chicken will continue to cook as it rests. Turn the heat off under the oil in the meantime.
5 Reheat the oil to 355°F (180°C) and put the chicken back in for another minute or so. When the surface is crisp, remove the chicken and drain on fresh paper towels. Serve garnished with the shredded cabbage.

CRISPY CHICKEN NUGGETS with SWEET-SOUR ORANGE GLAZE

Try serving this dish with half of the chicken pieces coated in this delicious sweet-sour sauce.

SERVES 2-4

2 tablespoons orange marmalade
2 tablespoons rice vinegar

Combine the marmalade and vinegar in a large bowl. Add half of the chicken from step 5 above and mix to coat. Arrange a serving plate with the rest of the chicken and the shredded cabbage.

CRUNCHY CURRIED CHICKEN GIZZARDS

The crunchiness of the gizzards, the exotic accent of curry spices and the
fragrance of garlic characterize this izakaya favorite.

SERVES 2

8 oz (225 g) chicken gizzards
2 tablespoons cornstarch
Oil for deep-frying
2 lemon slices

FOR THE MARINADE
½ teaspoon minced garlic
2 teaspoons curry powder
2 teaspoons soy sauce
¼ teaspoon sea salt, or
    to taste

1 Cut each gizzard in half. Make 4 shallow
crosswise cuts into each piece and remove
any sinew.
2 Put the gizzards into a bowl, add the
marinade ingredients and rub them into the
meat with your hands. Cover with plastic
wrap and refrigerate for 5 minutes. Coat
with the cornstarch, shaking off any excess.
3 Heat the frying oil to 355°F (180°C) and
put in the chicken gizzards. Fry for about
3 minutes, turning occasionally. When
they are browned and crispy, transfer to
a paper-towel-lined plate to drain the oil.
Serve on two individual plates, each ac-
companied by a slice of lemon.

Make shallow cuts halfway into each
gizzard piece ¼ in (6 mm) apart. The
flavors will penetrate better, and the
gizzards easier to eat.

HONEY SESAME CHICKEN WINGS

A sweet-savory sauce with honey and lots of fragrant sesame seeds defines this delicious Nagoya speciality.

SERVES 2

8 chicken wingettes (the middle
    joint of the chicken wing)
⅓ teaspoon sea salt
2 tablespoons cornstarch
Oil for deep-frying
1 tablespoon roasted sesame seeds

FOR THE SAUCE

4 tablespoons soy sauce
2½ tablespoons mirin (see note,
    page 11)
1½ tablespoon sake
1½ tablespoon honey

1 Combine the sauce ingredients in a pan and stir well. Place over medium heat and bring to a boil, then remove from the heat.
2 Make an incision in each chicken wingette along the bone with a sharp knife. Sprinkle with the salt, then coat with the cornstarch. Shake off any excess.
3 Heat the oil to 355°F (180°C). Add the prepared chicken wingettes and deep-fry for about 7 minutes, turning occasionally. When the wingettes are browned and crispy, transfer to a paper-towel-lined plate to drain.
4 Place the chicken in a bowl, add the sauce from step 1 and the sesame seeds and mix well to coat. Arrange on a serving plate.

Cut into the chicken along the bone so that the meat cooks evenly.

PORK and ONION SKEWERS

The breadcrumb coating for these skewers is flavored with parsley and grated cheese, making for an original twist on this izakaya favorite.

4 SKEWERS

8 oz (225 g) boneless pork shoulder cutlets
1 onion
1 teaspoon sea salt, or to taste
Black pepper, to taste
6 tablespoons flour
2 beaten eggs
Oil for deep-frying
2 tablespoons whole-grain mustard

FOR THE SEASONED BREADCRUMBS
2 teaspoons finely chopped flat-leaf parsley
1 teaspoon grated Parmesan cheese
4 tablespoons soft breadcrumbs

1 Slice the pork crosswise (perpendicular to the grain of the meat) into four equally sized pieces. Cut the onion into eight wedges. Skewer the pork and onion alternately onto two skewers (alternating one piece of pork with two pieces of onion and so on). Season with the salt and pepper.
2 Mix the seasoned breadcrumb ingredients together well on a flat plate.
3 Heat the oil to 340°F (170°C). Dip the pork-and-onion skewers into the flour, beaten egg and the seasoned breadcrumbs, in that order.
4 When the oil is hot, place the skewers in a strainer or spider skimmer and deep-fry for about 5 minutes, turning occasionally. When they are lightly browned and crispy, transfer to a paper-towel-lined plate to drain. Arrange on a serving plate with the mustard on the side.

STUFFED LOTUS ROOT SKEWERS

The holes of the lotus root are stuffed with mentaiko roe before frying. This skewer with a spicy kick is one you definitely want to add to your repertoire.

2 SKEWERS

2-in (5-cm) piece lotus root (see note, page 11)
Pinch of salt
3 tablespoons mentaiko roe (see note, page 11)
6 tablespoons flour
2 beaten eggs
4 tablespoons soft breadcrumbs
Oil for deep-frying

1 Peel the lotus root. Place in a pan with the salt and add water to cover. Bring to a boil over high heat, then turn the heat down to low and boil for about 3 minutes. Drain the lotus root, pat dry and pierce with two skewers placed at equal distances along the lotus root.
2 Cut into the membrane of the mentaiko sac and scrape out the eggs inside with a knife. Stuff the mentaiko into the holes of the lotus root. Dip the lotus root into the flour, beaten egg and breadcrumbs, in that order.
3 Heat the frying oil to 375°F (190°C). Place the lotus root in a strainer or spider skimmer and deep-fry, turning occasionally, for about 3 minutes. When it is lightly browned and crispy, transfer to a paper-towel-lined plate to drain the oil. Cut through the lotus root in between the skewers to make two slices and arrange on a serving plate.

TORN CABBAGE SALAD

A little bit of salt and nutty sesame oil really enhance the sweetness of the cabbage.

SERVES 2

2 large cabbage leaves
Pinch of sea salt, to taste
½ teaspoon sesame oil

Tear the cabbage leaves into coarse pieces with your hands and arrange on a serving plate. Sprinkle with the salt and sesame oil.

CAMEMBERT SKEWERS

These piping hot, gooey melted cheese skewers are irresistible!

2 SKEWERS

4 oz (125 g) Camembert
3 tablespoons flour
1 beaten egg
2 tablespoons soft breadcrumbs
Oil for deep-frying

1 Cut the Camembert into 4 equal wedges. Thread two wedges on two skewers. Wet the white rind side of the cheese with a little water. Dip the skewers in flour, beaten egg and breadcrumbs, in that order.

2 Heat the oil to 375°F (190°C). Place the skewers in a strainer or spider skimmer and deep-fry for about 3 minutes, turning occasionally. When they are lightly browned and crispy, transfer to a paper-towel-lined plate to drain, then arrange on a serving plate.

TARO and POTATO CROQUETTES

What makes this version of the classic potato croquette stand out is the use of two kinds of root vegetable—taro, which you can find in Asian groceries, and potatoes. Sautéed bacon and onions are added to multiply the deliciousness.

MAKES 4 CROQUETTES

2 taro roots, about 8 oz (225 g) total
1 potato
1 tablespoon water
3 thick bacon strips, about 3 oz (85 g) total
1 onion, peeled
¼ teaspoon sea salt, or to taste
Black pepper, to taste
Flour for dipping
1 beaten egg
Panko breadcrumbs, for coating
Oil for deep-frying
4 sprigs watercress

1 Peel and quarter the taro roots. Peel the potato and cut in half, then cut each half into four pieces. Put the taro and potato in a microwave-safe bowl with 1 tablespoon water, cover loosely with plastic wrap and microwave for about 10 minutes.

2 When a skewer goes through a piece of taro easily, they are done. Mash them up with the back of a fork.

3 Dice the bacon and the onion. Put the bacon in a frying pan and sauté over low heat for about 5 minutes. When the fat has rendered out, raise the heat to medium and add the onion. Sauté for another 3 minutes or so.

4 When the onion is lightly browned, take the frying pan off the heat and add the contents to the mashed taro and potato. Mix well with a fork. Add the salt and black pepper and mix well again.

5 Divide the filling into four equal portions and form each into a ball. Dip each ball into the flour, beaten egg and panko breadcrumbs, in that order.

6 Heat the oil to 355°F (180°C). Deep-fry the croquettes for about 2 minutes, turning occasionally. When they are browned and crispy, transfer to a paper-towel-lined plate to drain. Serve the watercress alongside.

JAPANESE-STYLE CRUNCHY FRIED CHICKEN CUTLETS

Called *yurinchi* in Japan, this is a Japanese version of the crispy fried chicken that is popular in Cantonese and Hong Kong cuisine. A vinegar-based sauce with lots of aromatic vegetables is poured over the chicken while it's still sizzling hot.

SERVES 2

2 boneless chicken thighs, skin on
1 teaspoon sea salt, or to taste
Black pepper to taste
3 tablespoons cornstarch
Oil for deep-frying

FOR THE SAUCE

4-in (10-cm) length Japanese or baby leek, or thick green onion (white part only), trimmed and finely chopped
½ teaspoon finely minced garlic (see page 7)
½ teaspoon peeled and finely chopped fresh ginger
3 tablespoons water
3 tablespoons rice vinegar
3 tablespoons sugar
2 tablespoons sesame oil

1 Combine the sauce ingredients in a bowl and mix well to blend.
2 Use a sharp knife to make several incisions in the chicken on the skinless side, severing the muscle fibers. This prevents the meat from shrinking when it's fried.
3 Season the chicken with the salt and pepper, then coat both sides well with cornstarch. Shake off any excess.
4 Heat the oil to 355°F (180°C). Put in the chicken, skin side down, and fry for about 7 minutes. Turn over and fry for another 3 minutes or so.
5 When the chicken is browned and crispy, transfer to a paper-towel-lined plate to drain and let rest for about a minute. Cut into bite-sized pieces, arrange on a serving plate, and pour the sauce from step 1 over all.

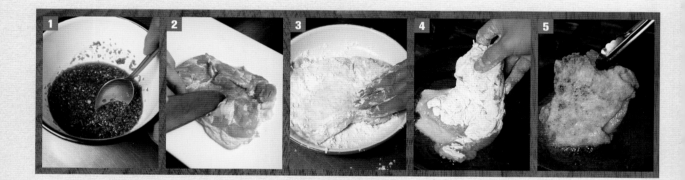

CRISPY FRIED MACKEREL FILLETS

The Japanese name of this classic dish, tatsuta-age, is said to be inspired by the river Tatsuta in Nara prefecture. The reddish-brown surface of the fried mackerel, broken up by the bubbly white of the cornstarch, is reminiscent of fall leaves floating on the surface of the water. The radish and chili garnish, a classic accompaniment to many Japanese dishes, is called momiji-oroshi, meaning "grated red maple leaves."

SERVES 2

1 mackerel, deboned and filleted, about 8 oz (225 g)*
3 tablespoons cornstarch
Oil for deep-frying
½ red Thai chili pepper
1-in (3-cm) piece daikon radish (see note, page 11)

FOR THE MARINADE

1 teaspoon minced fresh ginger
1 teaspoon minced garlic
1 tablespoon soy sauce
1 tablespoon sake

1 Pat the mackerel dry with paper towels and cut each fillet into three pieces. Combine the marinade ingredients in a bowl and mix well. Add the mackerel pieces, stir to coat and leave for about 15 minutes.

2 Deseed the chili pepper. Peel the daikon radish, poke a hole through the middle with a chopstick and insert the chili pepper. Grate into a fine-meshed sieve and leave to drain.

3 Coat the mackerel pieces generously with cornstarch. Shake off the excess.

4 Heat the oil to 340°F (170°C). Fry the mackerel for about 3 minutes, turning occasionally.

5 When the mackerel is browned and crispy, transfer to a paper-towel-lined plate to drain. Arrange on a serving plate with the grated daikon radish.

*Try using other boneless filleted fish instead of the mackerel. You can use white fish like cod or sea bass–or salmon, for a very different version of this dish. I also recommend trying this recipe with lean pork fillet, chicken breast meat, chicken tenders and so on, since the marinade adds flavor and richness to such low-fat cuts. All versions taste good when they're cold, so they're great in bento boxes.

BEER-BATTERED SMELTS with NORI SEAWEED PASTE

Nori seaweed paste and beer are added to the batter for a light, crispy texture. A bite of this will gently fill your senses with the flavors and fragrance of the sea.

SERVES 2

8 whole smelts, about 6 oz (170 g) total, well chilled
1 tablespoon nori seaweed paste*
5 tablespoons flour
⅓ cup (85 ml) cold beer
Oil for deep-frying
1 wedge lemon

*Nori Seaweed Paste Called *nori no tsukudani* in Japanese, this is a dark brown, almost black paste made with nori seaweed and added flavors. It is available at Japanese grocery stores in small jars. If you can't get it, try making your own by shredding a couple of sheets of nori seaweed and simmering in a little water, soy sauce, sugar and mirin until it forms a thick paste.

1 Put the flour and nori seaweed paste in a bowl and add the cold beer. Whisk until smooth.
2 Heat the oil to 355°F (180°C). Holding each smelt by the head so the it remains uncoated, dip into the batter and then put into the oil. Fry for about 3 minutes, turning occasionally. When the fish are brown and crispy, transfer to a paper-towel-lined plate to drain. Arrange on a serving plate with the lemon wedge.

Chilled beer makes the batter crisp and crunchy.

STUFFED MACKEREL FRITTERS

The tart umeboshi salted plums and fragrant shiso leaves used in the stuffing, and the umami of the fish combine to create a perfect symphony of flavors.

SERVES 2

2 mackerel, sardines or similarly sized blue fish, about 8 oz (225 g) total
¼ teaspoon sea salt
1 umeboshi salted plum, soft type (see note, page 12)
2 green shiso leaves (see note, page 12)
2 tablespoons flour
1 beaten egg
Panko breadcrumbs, for coating
Oil for deep-frying
Pinch of fine bonito flakes (see note, page 11)
2 tablespoons mayonnaise

1 Open up the fish from the back (see page 9 for method) and salt both sides. Pit the umeboshi and chop the flesh into a paste with a knife. Remove the stems from the shiso.

2 Spread an equal amount of ume paste over the inner sides of each fish and top with a shiso leaf each. Close up the fish so that the ume and shiso are in the middle. Dip each fish in the flour, beaten egg and breadcrumbs, in that order.

3 Heat the frying oil to 355°F (180°C). Add the breaded fish and fry for about 3 minutes, turning occasionally. When the fish is browned and crispy, take it out and transfer to a paper-towel-lined plate to drain. Arrange on a serving plate. Mix the bonito flakes and mayonnaise together and serve on the side as a sauce.

Arrange the shiso leaf so that it covers the inner sides of the fish evenly.

SQUID FRITTERS with STEAK SAUCE

The key to these delicious fritters is the combination of the two different textures
of squid—the chopped-up squid made into a paste and the chewy legs.

SERVES 2

1 fresh squid, about 9 oz (260 g)
¼ onion, finely chopped (see page 7 for method)
1 teaspoon panko breadcrumbs
¼ teaspoon sea salt, or to taste
Pinch of black pepper
2 tablespoons flour
1 beaten egg
Panko breadcrumbs, for coating
Oil for deep-frying
2 tablespoons Japanese Worcester-shire steak sauce*

FOR THE GARNISH

2 lettuce leaves, shredded
Small piece carrot, cut into match-sticks (see page 6)
Small piece daikon radish (see note, page 11), cut into matchsticks

*Japanese Worcestershire Steak Sauce
Usually just called "sauce" in Japan, this brown condiment is thicker and sweeter than its British equivalent, and similar to HP steak sauce. It is used on fried foods, hamburger steaks, as a flavoring ingredient for fried noodles, and more. It is available at Japanese grocery stores; the most popular brand has a bulldog as the logo. **Okonomiyaki sauce,** used on okonomiyaki savory pancakes, is simi-lar. Steak sauce can be substituted although the taste is distinctly different.

1 Clean and cut up the squid (see page 8). Peel off the flaps that stick out at the sides from the top of the squid. Peel off a strip of the skin.
2 Use a paper towel to pinch the edge of the remaining skin and peel all the skin off the body and the flaps.
3 Cut the legs into ½-in (1-cm) pieces. Cut open the body so that it lies flat in one large piece, and remove ¼ in (6 mm) from all four edges. Do the same for the flaps. Chop the body and flaps finely until they turn into a paste (use a food processor if you like).
4 Place the squid paste and legs and the chopped onion in a bowl. Add the 1 teaspoon of panko breadcrumbs and the salt and pepper, and mix well to combine.
5 Divide the mixture into four equal portions and form into patties. Dip in the flour, beaten egg and panko breadcrumbs, in that order.
6 Heat the oil to 355°F (180°C) and put in the breaded patties. Fry for about 4 minutes, turning occasionally. When they are browned and crispy, transfer to a paper-towel-lined plate to drain. Arrange on a serving plate with the garnish vegetables. Have the sauce on the side to pour over the fritters before eating.

CRISPY NOODLE-WRAPPED FRIED SHRIMP

Somen, the thinnest of Japanese noodles, are made of wheat flour. They are sold in packets containing small bundles of dried noodles; find them at your Asian grocery.

SERVES 2

1 bundle somen noodles, about 2 oz (60 g)
2 large shrimp
Oil for deep-frying
2 tablespoons mentsuyu ready-made noodle sauce (the "straight-up" type, not the concentrated type)

FOR THE "GLUE"

1 tablespoon flour
1 tablespoon cornstarch
1½ tablespoons water

1 Bring a generous amount of water to a boil in a pan. Add the somen noodles and boil for about a minute. Drain into a colander, plunge into a bowl of cold water and swish them around in the water while rubbing them gently with your hands. Drain again and pat the noodles dry.

2 Devein one shrimp and remove the shell, leaving the tail and a small bit of shell above it still attached. Make three shallow cuts in the belly side of the shrimp, then put it on a cutting board and pull gently to straighten. Cut a small slice off the end of the tail and press the tail gently with the blade of a knife to squeeze out any liquid in the body. Repeat with the other shrimp.

3 Combine the "glue" ingredients in a bowl and mix well.

4 Coat each shrimp with the "glue," then wrap the somen noodles around the body several times.

5 Heat the oil to 355°F (180°C). Fry the shrimp for about 3 minutes, turning occasionally. When the somen noodles are browned and crispy, transfer to a paper-towel-lined plate to drain. Arrange on a serving plate with the mentsuyu on the side for dipping.

Leave the tails uncovered when you wrap the shrimp.

SCALLOP FRITTERS with SHISHITO PEPPERS

Burdock root, called gobo in Japanese, is sold at Asian supermarkets. If you can't find it, carrots, cabbage stems, or peeled broccoli stems have a similar texture, although the taste will be different.

SERVES 2

2-in (5-cm) length burdock root (see note, above)
2 shishito peppers*
2 large fresh scallops
Oil for deep-frying
Pinch of sea salt, to taste

FOR THE "GLUE"

1 tablespoon flour
1 tablespoon cornstarch
1½ tablespoons water

*Shishito Peppers These are very mild Japanese peppers, usually eaten while still green. You can find them at Japanese and Korean grocery stores, as well as some farmers' markets and supermarkets. Padron peppers are a good substitute.

1 Scrape the skin from the burdock root with a stiff vegetable brush and rinse with water. Use a vegetable peeler to sliver the burdock into a bowl of water. Let stand for about 3 minutes, then drain and pat dry.
2 Pierce the side of each shishito pepper with a knife. Combine the "glue" ingredients in a bowl and mix well.
3 Heat the oil to 355°F (180°C). Fry the shishito peppers for about a minute. When they turn bright green, take them out and set them on a paper-towel-lined plate to drain. Maintain the oil at the same temperature.
4 Coat the scallops with the "glue" and the slivered burdock root. Fry in the oil for about 3 minutes, turning occasionally. When the burdock root is crisp, transfer to the paper-towel-lined plate. Sprinkle with the salt and serve with the shishito peppers.

Rinsing the slivered burdock root in water will reduce any harshness.

CHIKUWA FISH CAKE FRITTERS with AONORI SEAWEED

Fritters with aonori powder, made from nori seaweed, are called isobe-age (seashore fritters). The seaside fragrance of the aonori gives them a special flavor.

SERVES 2

2 chikuwa grilled fish cakes (see note, page 11), or Thai fish cakes
Oil for deep-frying*

FOR THE BATTER

1 tablespoon aonori seaweed powder (see note, page 62)
3 tablespoons water
2½ tablespoons flour
Pinch of sea salt, to taste

1 Slice the fish cake into ¾-in (2-cm) pieces.
2 Combine the batter ingredients in a bowl and whisk until smooth.
3 Heat the oil to 355°F (180°C). Dip the fish cake pieces in the batter and drop into the oil. Fry for about 2 minutes, turning occasionally. When the pieces are lightly browned and crispy, transfer to a paper-towel-lined plate to drain. Arrange on a serving plate with some toothpicks.

Cover the fish cake pieces in batter and deep-fry.

*The temperature of the oil for deep-frying depends on the ingredients. Raw ingredients that take time to cook through, like potatoes and other starchy root vegetables, should be fried at a lower temperature (300–320°F/150–160°C). At this temperature, batter dropped in the oil sinks to the bottom and slowly rises to the surface. Use medium-temperature oil (340–355°F/170– 180°C) for items like thickly cut pork skewers. At this temperature, batter dropped in the oil floats back to the surface before it hits the bottom of the pan. Use hot oil (355–400°F/180–190°C) for things like tempura where you want a crispy finish. At this temperature, batter dropped in the oil will bounce back to the surface quickly.

SPICY FRIED OCTOPUS NUGGETS

The precooked octopus is flavored with garlic, paprika powder, chili powder and soy sauce before being quick-fried. The piquancy of the fried lemon creates a perfect balance of flavors.

SERVES 2

1 boiled octopus leg for sashimi,*
    about 5 oz (140 g)
½ lemon
1 tablespoon cornstarch
Oil for deep-frying
Pinch of sweet paprika powder

FOR THE SEASONING
¼ teaspoon minced garlic
½ teaspoon sweet paprika powder
¼ teaspoon sea salt, or to taste
¼ teaspoon black pepper
Pinch of red chili powder

*Octopus legs that have been treated and boiled to be served as sashimi are available at Japanese grocery stores.

1 Slice the octopus into ¾-in (2-cm) wide pieces and place in a bowl. Add the seasoning ingredients and mix well. Cover the bowl with plastic wrap and refrigerate for about 5 minutes.
2 Heat a frying pan over medium heat. Put in the lemon half, cut side down, and cook for about 3 minutes, until lightly browned.
3 Dust the octopus pieces with the cornstarch. Heat the oil to 355°F (180°C) and fry the octopus for about 2 minutes, turning occasionally. When the octopus pieces are browned and crispy, transfer to a paper-towel-lined plate to drain. Arrange on a serving plate, sprinkle with paprika powder and serve the browned lemon half on the side.

TOFU FRITTERS with EDAMAME

These fritters, called takoyaki in Japanese, contain a delicious mixture of tofu, hijiki seaweed and edamame beans. The dipping sauce is the classic clear, slightly thick gin-an sauce used in Japanese cooking.

MAKES 16

1 piece firm silken tofu, about 12 oz (350 g)
Handful dried hijiki seaweed (see note, page 57)
8 oz (225 g) unshelled edamame pods, fresh or frozen (see recipe headnote, page 16)
Sea salt, for rubbing
1 egg
4 oz (125 g) grated yamatoimo (see recipe headnote, page 62) or Chinese yam (see note, page 11)
½ tablespoon sugar
½ teaspoon sea salt
Oil for deep-frying*

FOR THE DIPPING SAUCE

2 tablespoons cornstarch
2 cups (500 ml) dashi stock (see page 6)
1 tablespoon soy sauce
½ tablespoon sugar
½ tablespoon mirin (see note, page 11)
¼ teaspoon sea salt, or to taste
Pinch of fresh minced ginger

1 Wrap the tofu in a piece of unbleached and undyed cheesecloth or muslin. Set a board or tray on top of the wrapped tofu and weight it with a bowl containing about a cup (250 ml) water. Leave for an hour to drain.
2 Rinse the hijiki seaweed. Place in a bowl with enough water to cover and let stand for about 20 minutes to reconstitute, then drain.
3 Bring a generous amount of water to a boil in a pan. In the meantime, unwrap the tofu, break in half, and mash into a smooth paste by passing it through a fine-mesh sieve.
4 If using fresh edamame, cut off both ends of each edamame pod with kitchen scissors, sprinkle the pods with a little salt and rub it in. Add the edamame to the pan of boiling water and cook for about 3 minutes. Drain, plunge into ice water and drain again. Shell the edamame and peel the thin skin off each bean before adding to the mashed tofu.
5 Add the soaked and drained hijiki, egg, grated yamatoimo or Chinese yam, sugar and salt to the tofu in step 4 and mix until smooth.
6 If you have a takoyaki maker, follow the instructions below.* If not, divide the tofu mixture into 16 equal portions, form each portion into a ball, and deep-fry in oil heated to 355°F (180°C), turning occasionally, for about 5 minutes. When evenly browned, transfer to a paper-towel-lined plate to drain, then arrange on a serving plate.
7 For the sauce, dissolve the cornstarch in 3 tablespoons of the dashi stock. Combine in a pan with the rest of the dipping sauce ingredients except for the minced ginger, place over medium heat and cook, stirring constantly. When the sauce thickens, transfer to a serving bowl and add the minced ginger. Dip the tofu fritters in the sauce to eat.

*If you have a takoyaki maker (the traditional grill pan used to make takoyaki octopus balls) you can use it instead of the deep-frying method in step 6. Heat some vegetable oil in the wells of the takoyaki maker, and pour in the mixture from step 5. When it starts to firm up, turn the balls over using a spoon while patting them into shape, so that they become evenly formed and are fried on all sides. When lightly browned, pour in about a teaspoon of oil into each well from the side. Flip the balls over so that they continue to shallow-fry. When they are evenly browned, transfer to a serving plate. You can buy takoyaki makers online and from well-stocked Japanese grocery stores.

Turn the balls over using a spoon.

When evenly browned, transfer to a serving plate.

YAM and NATTO FRITTERS WRAPPED in NORI

Natto (fermented soybeans) is quite pungent and sticky, but a taste worth acquiring for its health benefits. It's made with whole or split (hikiwari) soybeans of various sizes. Natto is available at Japanese grocery stores and some health food stores. Yamatoimo, a type of Chinese yam, has a pleasingly thick and chewy texture.

SERVES 2

4 oz (125 g) yamatoimo*
⅓ cup (60 g) small-bean natto (see note, above)
2 tablespoons flour
Pinch of sea salt
1 large sheet toasted nori seaweed, approx 7 x 8 in (18 x 20 cm)
Oil for deep-frying
1 teaspoon wasabi paste
1 tablespoon soy sauce

*If you can't find yamatoimo, use Chinese yam and add 1½–2 tablespoons of cornstarch after grating to make it thicker. If the batter is still too loose, try shallow-frying the fritters in a frying pan instead. See more about Chinese yam on page 11.

1 Peel the yamatoimo and grate it into a bowl. Add the natto, flour and salt, and mix well with a spoon.
2 Cut the nori sheet into 8 equally sized pieces.
3 Heat the oil to 355°F (180°C). Divide the mixture into 8 equal portions. Put each portion on a piece of nori, fold the nori over and drop into the oil. Fry, turning occasionally, for about 2 minutes. When the fritters are crispy on the outside, take them out and drain off the oil. Dip into soy sauce and wasabi to eat.

Fold the nori around the filling and carefully drop the fritters into the oil.

DEEP-FRIED TOFU in DASHI SAUCE

The soft tofu, the silky-smooth nameko mushrooms and the subtly sweet sauce all come together in perfect harmony in this classic dish.

SERVES 2

1 piece firm silken tofu, about 12 oz (350 g)

⅓ cup (85 g) cooked nameko mushrooms (canned, vacuum-packed or in a jar)*

2-in (5-cm) length daikon radish (see note, page 11)

⅛ teaspoon minced fresh ginger

2 tablespoons cornstarch

Oil for deep-frying

½ cup (125 ml) dashi stock (see page 6)

4 teaspoons mirin (see note, page 11)

4 teaspoons soy sauce

Shredded nori seaweed, to garnish

1 Pat the tofu dry and cut into 4 pieces. Put the mushrooms in a colander, rinse and drain. Peel the daikon radish, grate into a fine-mesh sieve and leave to drain.

2 Coat the tofu pieces with cornstarch and shake off the excess. Heat the oil to 355°F (180°C) and fry the tofu for about 3 minutes, turning occasionally. When the tofu is brown and crispy, transfer to a paper-towel-lined plate to drain.

3 Bring the dashi stock to a boil in a pan over medium heat. Add the mushrooms, grated daikon, mirin and soy sauce. Bring to a boil again, then remove from the heat and add the minced ginger.

4 Arrange the fried tofu on a serving plate and pour the sauce over it. Top with shredded nori seaweed.

Put the tofu carefully into the hot oil taking care not to let it crumble.

*Nameko mushrooms are small, light brown mushrooms with a slippery, gelatinous coating. They are often used in miso soup or as a topping. They are usually sold precooked and ready to eat in cans, vacuum-packed bags or jars. Some people prefer to give them a rinse before using, while others use them as is. You can find them in Japanese grocery stores.

IMPERIAL BEEF ROLLS

These Vietnamese morsels are called "imperial" to indicate they are the best.

MAKES 4 SPRING ROLLS

4 oz (125 g) boneless beef short rib
¼ carrot
2 large cabbage leaves
1 fresh shiitake mushroom
4 dried rice-paper spring roll wrappers
Oil for deep-frying
Lettuce and mint for garnish

FOR THE MARINADE
½ teaspoon sea salt, or to taste
½ teaspoon soy sauce
½ teaspoon fish sauce

FOR THE SAUCE
¼ thinly sliced green chili pepper
Pinch minced garlic
2 tablespoons fish sauce
2 tablespoons water
1½ tablespoons sugar
1½ tablespoons freshly squeezed lime
   or lemon juice

1 Cut the beef into ¼ x ¼ in (6 x 6 mm) wide strips. Peel the carrot, slice thinly on the diagonal, and then cut into ¼-in (6-mm) strips. Stack the cabbage leaves together, roll them up and cut into ¼-in (6-mm) strips. Remove the stem from the shiitake mushroom and slice the cap into ¼-in (6-mm) strips.

2 Combine all ingredients from step 1 in a bowl. Add the marinade ingredients and mix well by hand.

3 Run a rice-paper wrapper through water and place it on a damp kitchen towel. Put a quarter of the filling on the part closest to you. Fold the near edge of the wrapper over the filling, fold the sides in and roll up.

4 Heat the frying oil to 355°F (180°C). Fry the rolls for about 3 minutes, turning occasionally. When lightly browned and crispy, transfer to a paper-towel-lined plate to drain. Arrange on a serving plate with the lettuce and mint leaves. Mix the sauce ingredients together in a separate bowl to pour over the rolls before eating.

VEGETARIAN SPRING ROLLS

Okara is what's left of soybeans after the milk is extracted for tofu. It's high in fiber and protein. Find it at Japanese grocery stores—or at a tofu maker's, if you're lucky enough to live near one.

MAKES 4 SPRING ROLLS

3 slices dried shiitake mushroom*
2 tablespoons water
2 teaspoons sesame oil
Small bunch chives, about 1 oz (30 g),
    cut into 1-in (3-cm) pieces
Small piece carrot, cut into matchsticks
Pinch of sea salt
¼ cup (60 g) okara soy pulp (see note, above)
¼ teaspoon minced fresh ginger
2 teaspoons sake
1 teaspoon soy sauce
4 spring roll wrappers
Oil for deep-frying
1 teaspoon flour
1 teaspoon water

*If you can't find pre-cut dried shiitake mushrooms, use one whole dried shiitake mushroom, soak until it's soft enough to slice, then cut off a few slices to use in this recipe. Use the rest in another dish, and reserve 2 tablespoons of the soaking liquid to use here.

1 Soak the shiitake in the 2 tablespoons water for 20 minutes. Drain, reserving the soaking water.
2 Heat the sesame oil in a frying pan over medium heat, add the chives and carrot, sprinkle with the salt, and stir-fry for 1 minute. When the chives turn limp, add the okara and minced ginger and continue to stir-fry.
3 Add the shiitake mushroom soaking liquid, the sake and the soy sauce, and turn the heat to low. Simmer while stirring for about 5 minutes until there is very little liquid left in the pan. Take the mixture out of the pan and leave to cool.
4 Mix the flour and water in a bowl. Spread out one spring roll wrapper, and place a quarter of the filling on the part closest to you. Fold the near edge of the wrapper over the filling, and fold the sides in. Roll once from front to back, brush the flour-water on the edge and finish rolling. Repeat with the remaining wrappers.
5 Heat the frying oil to 355°F (180°C) and fry the spring rolls for 3 minutes, turning occasionally. When lightly browned and crispy, transfer to a paper-towel-lined plate to drain. Arrange on a serving plate.

FRIED SMASHED POTATOES

Potatoes are first boiled in their jackets then crushed and deep-fried for a pleasing texture.

SERVES 2

2 potatoes*
Pinch of salt
Oil for deep-frying
Sea salt for sprinkling, to taste

*Try using one large sweet potato instead of the regular potatoes. Put the sweet potato on a microwave-safe dish, cover loosely with plastic wrap, and microwave for about 5 minutes. All you have to do then is crush it like you would the regular potatoes and deep-fry. In addition to the salt, try serving the potato sprinkled with ground cumin or curry powder, or some chopped fresh rosemary leaves.

1 Scrub the potatoes, remove the eyes and put them in a pan with a generous amount of water and the pinch of salt. Bring to a boil over high heat, then turn the heat to low and cook for about 20 minutes. Leave to cool in the cooking water for about 10 minutes, then drain.
2 Place the potatoes on a cutting board and crush them with the bottom of a bowl. Break up the crushed potato into large pieces.
3 Heat the frying oil to 340°F (170°C). Fry the crushed potato pieces for about 5 minutes, turning occasionally. When they are lightly browned and crispy, transfer to a paper-towel-lined plate to drain. Arrange on a serving plate and sprinkle with sea salt.

The potatoes are soft, so you only need to crush them gently.

Chapter 4

SIMMERED, STEAMED and SMOKED

This chapter includes dishes like Beef Tendon and Daikon Simmered in Soy, Ginger and Sake; Soy and Sake Honey-Glazed Ribs; and Spicy Octopus in Tomato Sauce. These recipes take some time and effort, but the flavors—as well as the sense of accomplishment you get—are unparalleled. In this chapter, you'll also find some home-smoking recipes to create that authentic izakaya flavor in your own kitchen!

PORK VARIETY MEATS SIMMERED in MISO, GINGER and SAKE

Pork variety meats, which include livers, hearts and kidneys, are simmered with vegetables in a red-miso and sugar broth. The meat takes on the flavor of the miso as well as the sweetness of the vegetables. The finishing touch is a sprinkle of shichimi togarashi, a seven-spice mix that includes red chili peppers, sesame seeds and citrus peel. You can find it at Japanese grocery stores and online.

SERVES 4

12 oz (350 g) mixed pork offal*
1 Japanese or baby leek, or thick green onion
4 cups (1 liter) plus 2 tablespoons water, divided
Handful pre-sliced dried shiitake mushroom (see note, page 89)
3-in (8-cm) length daikon radish (see note, page 11)
Shichimi togarashi (see note, above), to taste, or five-spice or red pepper powder

FOR THE SEASONING

1 small knob fresh ginger, peeled and minced
2 cloves garlic, minced
4 tablespoons sake
6 tablespoons red or other miso paste
4 tablespoons mirin (see note, page 11)
2 tablespoons sugar
1 teaspoon sea salt, or to taste

1 Rinse the offal under running water. Place in a pan with water to cover and bring to a boil over high heat. Drain in a colander and rinse with water again, then drain again.

2 Wash the pan and add the parboiled offal and green part of leek (reserving the white part), along with 4 cups (1 liter) of the water. Bring to a boil, reduce heat to low, and simmer for about 1 hour.

3 Place the sliced dried shiitake mushrooms and the remaining 2 tablespoons water in a bowl and soak for about 20 minutes to reconstitute. Reserve the soaking water.

4 Peel the daikon radish, cut into quarters lengthwise and then into slices 1-in (3-cm) thick. Put into a separate pan with water to cover and bring to a boil. Lower the heat and simmer for 10 minutes. Cool the daikon under running water; drain.

5 Remove the leek from the pan with the offal and transfer the remaining contents, including cooking liquid, to a heavy pan with thick sides. Add the shiitake and soaking liquid from step 3, as well as the daikon and carrot. Add all the seasoning ingredients and stir well to combine.

6 Cut a piece of kitchen parchment in a circle slightly larger than the circumference of the heavy pan and poke a hole in the middle. Use this as a drop lid to sit on top of the contents of the pan. Turn the heat to medium, and bring to a boil. Turn the heat to low, and simmer for 30 minutes. If it looks like the liquid is boiling off, add a little water. Top with the trimmed and sliced white part of the leek and sprinkle with shichimi togarashi before eating.

*In Japan you can buy a packet of cleaned mixed pork offal at the supermarket. It usually contains pieces of large and small intestine, liver, lungs, heart and sometimes stomach. It may be difficult to find a ready-made mix like this elsewhere, but ask your butcher what they can provide. Also try looking in Japanese, Chinese, Korean and Hispanic grocery stores.

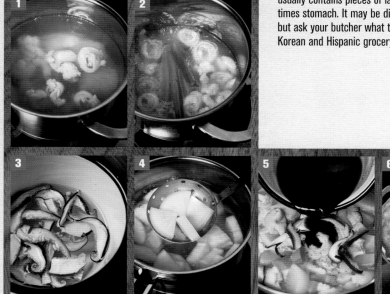

BEEF TENDON and DAIKON SIMMERED in SOY, GINGER and SAKE

Beef tendon is a cheap cut that's popular in many Asian cuisines. Though tough, it turns tender and gelatinous when cooked for a long time, and is very healthy. If you can't find beef tendon at your Asian grocery store, try substituting beef shank or oxtail.

SERVES 4

1 lb (500 g) beef tendon (see note, above)
8 cups (2 liters) water
2 Japanese or baby leeks, or thick green onions, green parts only
8-in (20-cm) length daikon radish (see note, page 11)
2 green onions (scallions) (green part only)

FOR THE SEASONING

1 knob fresh ginger, peeled and minced
1 cup (250 ml) water
½ cup (120 ml) soy sauce
6 tablespoons sake
3 tablespoons sugar

1 Cut the beef tendon into bite-sized pieces.
2 Put the beef tendon and the 4 cups (1 liter) water in a heavy pan over high heat. Just before it starts boiling, skim off the scum and add the green part of the leek. Turn the heat to low, and simmer for about an hour, skimming off the scum from time to time. Keep the heat low so that the broth doesn't become cloudy.
3 Peel the daikon radish and cut into bite-sized pieces. Put in a separate pan with enough water to cover. Bring to a boil over high heat, then lower the heat and simmer for 10 minutes. Cool under running water; drain.
4 Remove the green onion from the pan with the beef tendon. Add the daikon radish and all seasoning ingredients and stir well.
5 Cut a piece of kitchen parchment paper into a circle slightly larger than the circumference of the heavy pan and poke a hole in the middle. Use this as a drop lid so that the stew will cook evenly. Turn the heat to medium and bring to a boil, then turn the heat to low and simmer for about 40 minutes. Slice the green onion thinly and use as a garnish.

GLAZED PORK BELLY with SEASONAL GREENS

Pork belly cut into large chunks is simmered in a sweet-savory sauce until shiny, brown and tender.
The flavor and richness of the sauce are seductive and habit-forming—be warned!

SERVES 4

1 lb (500 g) whole pork belly
4 cups (1 liter) water
1 Japanese or baby leek, or thick
   green onion (green part only)
1 knob fresh ginger, peeled and
   thinly sliced
2 hard-boiled eggs
1 head baby bok choy, about 5 oz
   (140 g), or other seasonal greens
Pinch of salt
Karashi mustard, to taste*

FOR THE SEASONING

2 tablespoons sake
2 tablespoons mirin (see note,
   page 11)
2 tablespoons soy sauce
1½ tablespoons sugar

*Karashi Mustard Japanese karashi is a
spicy, smooth yellow mustard. If you can't
find it, English mustard is a good substitute.

1 Cut the pork into 4 pieces, put into a heavy pan with the water, and bring to a boil over high heat.
2 Skim off the scum as the water comes to a boil.
3 Add the leek and the sliced ginger to the pan. Turn the heat down to low and simmer the pork for about 45 minutes, skimming off the scum from time to time. If the water boils down below the level of the pork, add some more so that the pork is covered.
4 Remove the leek. Mix the seasoning ingredients together and add to the pan. Stir to combine.
5 Cut a piece of kitchen parchment paper in a circle slightly larger than the circumference of the pan and poke a hole in the middle. Use this as a drop lid to ensure the pan's contents will cook evenly. Turn the heat to medium, and bring to a boil. Turn the heat down to low, and simmer for about 15 minutes.
6 Add the whole hard-boiled eggs, replace the parchment paper insert and simmer for another hour or so. Turn off the heat and allow to stand for another hour, then skim off the fat from the surface.
7 Remove the parchment paper lid and place the pan over medium heat. Simmer, turning the pan occasionally to reduce the sauce and coat the pork, for about 15 minutes.
8 Halve the bok choy lengthwise. Place in a frying pan with the pinch of salt and a tablespoon of water, cover tightly and steam-cook for about 1 minute. Arrange the bok choy on a serving plate, top with the pork and eggs, and serve with mustard on the side.

SOY and SAKE HONEY-GLAZED RIBS

Add sautéed onions and minced ginger and garlic to the simmering broth for depth of flavor. You'll want to just grab these ribs with your hands to enjoy them.

SERVES 2-4

1 lb (500 g) pork spare ribs (6 to 7 ribs)
½ teaspoon sea salt, or to taste
Dash black pepper
½ onion, finely chopped (see page 7)
½ tablespoon vegetable oil

FOR THE SIMMERING BROTH

½ teaspoon minced fresh ginger
½ teaspoon minced garlic
1¾ cups (425 ml) water
2 tablespoons soy sauce
5 teaspoons sake
4 teaspoons mirin (see note, page 11)
4 teaspoons tablespoons honey
½ teaspoon white sesame seeds

1 Season the ribs on both sides with the salt and pepper. Heat the vegetable oil in a small frying pan over medium heat. Add the spare ribs and brown them for about 4 minutes, turning occasionally. When they are browned on all sides, remove them from the pan.
2 Heat the frying pan again over medium heat, add the onion and sauté for about 2 minutes. When the onion is lightly browned, add the simmering broth ingredients to the pan, along with the seared spare ribs from step 1. Bring to a boil, then turn heat to low and cover with a wooden drop lid or parchment cut as described on page 92. Simmer for about 30 minutes.
3 Remove the drop lid, raise the heat to medium and cook the ribs for an additional 10 minutes or so while rotating the pan occasionally so that the sauce in the pan coats the ribs. Transfer the ribs to a serving plate and pour any sauce left in the pan over them. Sprinkle the sesame seeds over.

Reduce the simmering broth, taking care not to scorch the ribs.

BEEF SIMMERED with TOFU and LEEK

In this dish, known as niku dofu in Japan, the tofu and leek both take on the umami of the beef that they are simmered with.

SERVES 2-4

12 oz (350 g) beef shank or chuck, thinly sliced

1 piece yaki-dofu (grilled tofu),* about 12 oz (350 g)

1 Japanese or baby leek, or thick green onion

½ tablespoon vegetable oil

FOR THE SIMMERING BROTH

1¼ cups (300 ml) dashi stock (see page 6)

2 tablespoons sake

2 tablespoons mirin (see note, page 11)

2 tablespoons soy sauce

1 tablespoon sugar

*If you can't find yaki-dofu at your Japanese grocery (see note, page 12) use regular firm tofu instead. After drying and cutting the tofu in step 1 and sautéing the leek in step 2, add the tofu cubes to the frying pan and fry until lightly brown. Turn over and brown on the other side.

1 Pat the yaki-dofu dry (if using regular firm tofu, drain as described on page 56, step 1). Cut into 8 squares. Slice the white part of the leek into 2-in (5-cm) lengths, and the green part into thin rounds.

2 Heat the vegetable oil in a small frying pan over medium heat. Add the white parts of the leek and sauté for about 2 minutes, stirring gently, until lightly browned. Remove from the pan.

3 Place the pan over medium heat and add about 1 oz (30 g) of the beef. Pan-fry one side until browned, and then add the simmering broth ingredients, the white part of the leek from step 2 and the tofu. Simmer over low heat for about 15 minutes.

4 Raise the heat to medium and add the rest of the beef and the green parts of the leek. When the liquid comes back to a boil, turn the heat down low, simmer for another minute or so, and transfer to a serving bowl.

The umami of the beef is transferred to the onion and the tofu.

AMBERJACK SIMMERED with DAIKON, SOY and GINGER

Using amberjack with the bones still in adds to the flavor of the broth and the fish. If you can't find precut amberjack, cut it up yourself or ask your fishmonger to do so. This dish is best in winter when mature amberjack (called buri in Japanese) are rich with fat.

SERVES 2-4

2-in (5-cm) length daikon radish
   (see note, page 11)
1 lb (500 g) amberjack pieces,
   bone-in
Pinch of sea salt
2 snow peas
Pinch of salt

FOR THE SIMMERING BROTH

1 small piece fresh ginger, peeled
   and cut into fine matchsticks
1 scant cup (200 ml) water
4 tablespoons soy sauce
2 tablespoons mirin (see note,
   page 11)

1 Peel the daikon radish and cut it in half crosswise. Bevel the edges of each piece.

2 Make several cuts about halfway through the thickness of the daikon radish pieces on one cut side, as shown in the photo.

3 Place the prepared daikon radish pieces in a pan with enough water to cover and bring to a boil over high heat. Reduce heat to low and cook for about 20 minutes. When the daikon has turned translucent, drain into a colander and cool under running water. Drain again.

4 Sprinkle the amberjack pieces with the salt and line them up on a shallow tray or plate. Cover with plastic wrap and refrigerate for about 5 minutes. Bring a generous amount of water to a boil and add the amberjack pieces. Parboil over medium heat for about a minute. When the fish has turned white, remove from the pot and rinse them well with plenty of water. Pat dry with paper towels. (Parboiling eliminates the strong fishy flavor of mature amberjack.)

5 Combine the simmering broth ingredients in a pan and add the parboiled daikon radish and amberjack. Cut a piece of kitchen parchment paper in a circle slightly larger than the circumference of the heavy pan and poke a hole in the middle. Use this as a drop lid to ensure the pan's contents will cook evenly. Bring to a boil over medium heat, then reduce the heat to low and simmer for about 20 minutes.

6 Remove the strings from the snow peas. Bring some water to a boil in a separate pan and add the pinch of salt. Add the snow peas and blanch briefly, then cool under running water. Slice thinly on the diagonal. Arrange the daikon radish on two serving plates, top with the amberjack and pour any sauce left in the pan over all. Garnish with the snow peas.

TUNA SLOW POACHED in OLIVE OIL

Sashimi-grade lean tuna is poached gently at low temperature in olive oil. The flavors of the garlic, thyme and bay leaf in the oil are transferred to the fish, elevating it above the ordinary.

SERVES 2

½ clove garlic
8 oz (225 g) sashimi-grade tuna*
1½ teaspoons shio koji (see note, page 12)
1 sprig fresh thyme
1 bay leaf
1 scant cup (200 ml) olive oil
Baguette slices, for serving

*Sashimi-Grade Fish Raw sashimi-grade fish must be impeccably fresh. Make sure you buy your fish from a reputable store with a high product turnover. Ready-to-slice fish fillets that can be used for sashimi or sushi are available at Japanese grocery stores. Some large fish-mongers also carry sashimi-grade fish.

1 Slice the garlic thinly crosswise.
2 Pat the tuna dry with paper towels. Coat with the shio koji, then place the garlic, thyme and bay leaf on top and wrap tightly with plastic wrap. Refrigerate for 30 minutes.
3 Remove the plastic wrap and transfer the tuna to a small pan. Cover with the olive oil and simmer for about 5 minutes over low heat, swirling the pan around occasionally. When the tuna changes color, take the pan off the heat and continue cooking the tuna with the residual heat. Transfer to a serving plate and serve with some thinly sliced baguette on the side.

Put the tuna in cold oil to start with and cook slowly over low heat.

SARDINES SIMMERED in SAKE

Simmered fish prepared the old-fashioned way make a perfect drinking snack to serve at your home izakaya after a hard day at work. The bracing sourness of the pickled umeboshi plum somehow seems to soothe your tired soul.

SERVES 2

4 sardines, about 1 lb oz (500 g) total
2 umeboshi pickled plums, soft type (see note, page 12)
1 small knob fresh ginger

FOR THE SIMMERING BROTH
1 scant cup (200 ml) water
Scant ½ cup (100 ml) sake
2 tablespoons sugar
1 tablespoon mirin (see note, page 11)
1½ tablespoons soy sauce

1 Remove the scales and heads from the sardines. Cut a sliver off the belly sides and remove the innards (see page 10 for method). Wash out the insides and pat dry with paper towels. Peel the ginger. Slice half of it thinly and cut the other half into fine slivers.

2 Combine all the simmering broth ingredients in a heavy pan and stir well. Add the sardines, the thinly sliced ginger and the umeboshi. Cut a piece of kitchen parchment paper in a circle slightly larger than the circumference of the pan and poke a hole in the middle. Use this as a drop lid to ensure the pan's contents will cook evenly. Bring to a boil over medium heat, then lower the heat and simmer for about 10 minutes.

3 Remove the parchment-paper lid. Continue simmering for another 3 minutes or so, spooning the broth over the fish. Arrange on a serving plate and top with the slivered ginger.

Spoon the broth over the sardines while they simmer.

RUM RAISIN PUMPKIN

The sweet, tangy raisins and the rum add rich flavor to the kabocha squash, bringing out its natural sweetness. Butternut squash can also be used in this recipe.

SERVES 2-4

½ small kabocha or butternut
   squash, about 1 lb (500 g), pulp
   and seeds removed
2 tablespoons raisins or sultanas
1 teaspoon unsalted butter

FOR THE SIMMERING BROTH

1 scant cup (200 ml) water
1 teaspoon rum (or use whisky or
   brandy instead)
½ teaspoon sugar
½ teaspoon sea salt, or to taste

1 Cut the kabocha flesh into 1-in (3-cm) pieces. Bevel the sharp edges of the cut pieces. (This cutting method, called mentori, prevents the edges of simmered vegetables from disintegrating in the liquid as it cooks.)
2 Combine the kabocha, raisins and simmering broth ingredients in a small pan over medium heat. When the broth comes to a boil, reduce heat to low and cover with a drop lid or parchment cut as described in the recipe on page 92, step 6. Simmer for about 15 minutes.
3 Once a skewer goes through a piece of kabocha squash easily, take off the lid and add the butter. Simmer for an additional 5 minutes or so, swirling the pan every so often to coat the kabocha squash with the sauce. When the sauce has thickened, transfer the kabocha squash to a serving plate.

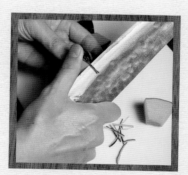

SPICY OCTOPUS in TOMATO SAUCE

Aromatic herbs give the tomato sauce a wonderful depth of flavor. The texture of the tender simmered octopus is wonderfully satisfying too.

SERVES 2

5 oz (140 g) boiled octopus leg for sashimi (see note, page 83)
½ onion
1 clove garlic
½ stalk celery
¼ medium carrot
1 tablespoon olive oil
Sea salt, for sprinkling
Pinch of ground chili pepper, to taste
⅛ teaspoon sea salt
2 tablespoons sake
½ cup (125 g) canned diced tomatoes
2 sprigs fresh thyme
1 sprig fresh rosemary, halved
2 tablespoons water
4 pitted green olives
Coarsely ground black pepper

1 Cut the octopus into ½-in (2-cm) wide slices. Finely chop the onion (see page 7), garlic and celery. Peel the carrot and chop finely.

2 Put the olive oil and chopped vegetables from step 1 into a frying pan, sprinkle with a little salt and sauté over low heat for about 5 minutes.

3 Add the octopus, ground chili pepper and the remaining salt to the pan and mix. Turn the heat to medium and sprinkle in the sake. Let the alcohol cook off.

4 Add the tomatoes, thyme, the rosemary sprig and the 2 tablespoons water to the pan and stir. Bring to a boil, then turn heat to low and simmer for about 15 minutes. When the octopus is tender, stir in the olives. Transfer to a serving plate and sprinkle with coarsely ground black pepper.

STEAMED SEA BREAM with MUSHROOMS and SPROUTS

This is a simple steamed dish that can be made in the microwave. The flavor-packed sauce with ginger and doubanjiang spicy bean paste is amazingly tasty.

SERVES 2

2 sea bream fillets, about 12 oz (350 g) total
Pinch each of sea salt and pepper
1 cup (100 g) bean sprouts
Small bunch enoki mushrooms, about 2 oz (60 g)
4-in (10-cm) length Japanese or baby leek, or thick green onion (white part only) trimmed
2 tablespoons sake

FOR THE SAUCE

8-in (20-cm) length leek or thick green onion (white part only) trimmed and roughly chopped*
½ teaspoon minced fresh ginger
2 tablespoons soy sauce
1 teaspoon vinegar
½ teaspoon doubanjiang spicy bean paste (see recipe headnote, page 124)

1 Pat the fish dry with paper towels and sprinkle both sides with salt and pepper. Remove the roots and caps from the bean sprouts. Put the sprouts in a colander and rinse under running water, then drain. Cut the hard roots from the stems of the enoki mushrooms and divide into small clumps. Shred the leek finely (see page 7 for method). Let stand in a bowl of cold water for 5 minutes, then drain and pat dry.

2 Divide the bean sprouts and enoki mushrooms between two microwave-safe plates. Place a piece of fish on each plate, then sprinkle with the sake, cover loosely with plastic wrap, and microwave for about 10 minutes.

3 Mix the sauce ingredients together in a bowl.

4 Remove the plastic wrap from the plates, divide the shredded leek from step 1 between the two plates, and pour the sauce over.

*Make several lengthwise cuts in the leek, then chop from one end.

SAKE-STEAMED PORK BELLY with FRESH VEGETABLES

Find ready-sliced pork-belly at a Japanese or Korean grocery, or make your own by freezing a block of pork belly for about an hour, then slicing it thinly. The delicious sesame dipping sauce is what really makes this dish special!

SERVES 2

2 green asparagus stalks
Small cluster shimeji mushrooms
1 small carrot
2-in (5-cm) length lotus root (see note, page 11)
2 small tomatoes
6 oz (170 g) thinly sliced pork belly (see note, above)
2 tablespoons sake

FOR THE SESAME SAUCE

1 tablespoon tahini
1 tablespoon ground sesame seeds
½ teaspoon sugar
½ teaspoon soy sauce
½ teaspoon mayonnaise
½ teaspoon rice vinegar

1 Peel the root end of the asparagus about a third of the way up and cut the stalk in half crosswise. Cut off the hard stem ends of the shimeji mushrooms and separate into small clumps. Slice the carrot thinly lengthwise. Peel the lotus root, slice thinly and rinse under running water in a colander; drain. Cut the tomato in half lengthwise and remove the core.

2 Cut a piece of kitchen parchment paper 10-in (25-cm) long and poke several holes in it with the tip of a knife. Line a bamboo steamer with the paper. Fold the pork slices in half and line them up on the paper, then arrange the vegetables around the meat. Sprinkle the sake over the pork and vegetables.

3 Bring water to a boil in the base of the steamer and place the steamer on top, tightly covered. Steam over medium heat for about 5 minutes. Place the steamer on a plate.

4 Combine the sesame sauce ingredients in a bowl and mix well. Transfer to a serving bowl and serve alongside the bamboo steamer.

SOY and SAKE-STEAMED CLAMS with BUTTER

Once the clams open up, add butter and soy sauce and finish off quickly. The added richness and fragrance make this dish irresistible.

SERVES 2

1 lb (500 g) fresh clams* in their shells, purged of sand

4-in (10-cm) length Japanese or baby leek, or thick green onion, roots trimmed

½ cup sake

2 teaspoons butter

2 teaspoons soy sauce

*This recipe uses asari clams, also called Japanese littleneck clams or Manila clams. If you can't find them at your Japanese grocery store, use any other small clams instead.

1 Rub the clams together in their shells under running water, then drain. Slice the green and white parts of the leek thinly.

2 Set a frying pan over medium heat and add the clams, leek and sake; cover. When the liquid comes to a boil, steam for about 2 minutes, shaking the pan gently.

3 As soon as the clams open, remove the lid and add the butter and soy sauce. Swirl the pan around to distribute the flavors, then transfer the clams to a serving plate.

If you cook the clams for too long, they'll get hard. As soon as they open, they are ready.

BAKED COD with SHIO KOJI, SHISO and YUZU

The cod is sprinkled with shio koji, a seasoning made from fermented rice, which adds saltiness and umami, as well as shiso leaves and yuzu citrus which add fragrance. Then it is baked in parchment. Yum!

SERVES 2

2 pieces cod, about 12 oz (350 g) total

1½ teaspoons shio koji (see note, page 12)

3 small tomatoes

4 green shiso leaves (see note, page 12)

4 pieces yuzu citrus peel, about ½-in (1-cm) square (see note, page 12)

2 teaspoons yuzu or lemon juice

2 tablespoons soy sauce

1 Pat the cod dry with paper towels and sprinkle the shio koji over. Remove a little of the top and bottom of the tomatoes, then cut in half. Cut the stems off the shiso leaves.

2 Preheat the oven to 430°F (220°C). Cut a 12-in (30-cm) long sheet of kitchen parchment paper in half. Place two tomato halves at the center of the diagonal of each piece of paper. Put the shiso leaves and the cod on top. Place one piece of yuzu peel on each pile. Sprinkle the sake over all.

3 Bring opposing corners of the parchment paper together over the contents and fold them together.

4 Twist each end of the papers tightly.

5 Place the packets on a baking sheet and steam-bake in the oven for about 15 minutes, then transfer to serving plates. Combine the yuzu juice and soy sauce and serve on the side. Open the packets and top with the remaining pieces of yuzu peel.

Twist the ends of the paper tightly so no moisture escapes.

SMOKING YOUR OWN MEATS and SEAFOOD at HOME

You can enjoy smoking food easily even at home. The results taste good because they're homemade, plus you can be assured of exactly what ingredients are used.

HOMEMADE SMOKED BACON

This bacon is amazingly smoky and juicy. Both the lean and fat parts are sweet and fragrant. The more time you take to make it, the better it tastes.

SERVES 2–4

1 lb (500 g) block pork belly
1 clove garlic
4 teaspoons sea salt, or to taste
2 teaspoons sugar
1–2 oz (30–55 g) cherrywood or hickory chips

FOR THE SEASONING
2 sprigs fresh thyme
4-in (10-cm) sprig fresh rosemary, halved
1 bay leaf, torn in half

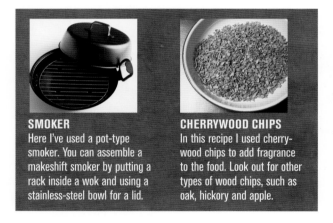

SMOKER
Here I've used a pot-type smoker. You can assemble a makeshift smoker by putting a rack inside a wok and using a stainless-steel bowl for a lid.

CHERRYWOOD CHIPS
In this recipe I used cherrywood chips to add fragrance to the food. Look out for other types of wood chips, such as oak, hickory and apple.

1 Thinly slice the garlic clove. Mix the salt and sugar together in a bowl. Put the pork on a shallow tray or plate and rub well with the salt-sugar mix.
2 Cover the surface of the pork with the garlic and herbs, and place in a resealable plastic bag. Remove as much air from the bag as you can, seal and refrigerate for 12–24 hours.
3 Remove and reserve the garlic and herbs from the pork and rinse the meat under running water to remove the salt on the surface. Place the pork in a bowl with water to cover and add the herbs and garlic. Let soak for about 2 hours to remove the salt.
4 Drain the pork, reserving the garlic and herbs, and pat dry with paper towels. Place the pork on a rack set over a shallow tray or similar, and put into a part of the refrigerator where it's exposed to cold air for about 24 hours to dry.
5 After drying the pork in the refrigerator, line the bottom of the smoker with aluminum foil and put in the wood chips. Set the rack, place the pork on top, cover with the lid and turn the heat on to high. When the wood chips start to smoke, reduce the heat to low and smoke for about an hour with the lid on. If the wood chips burn out, top with more as needed. When the bacon is nice and brown, transfer to a serving plate.

ASSORTED SMOKED SEAFOOD

Smoking scallops enhances their sweet flavor and really concentrates the umami. As for smoking fish, if you can find semi-dried fish at your Japanese grocery store, it's a lot easier.

SERVES 2-4

4 large fresh scallops
¼ teaspoon sea salt
2 lightly salted salmon fillets
4 whole semi-dried sardines
1 oz (30 g) cherrywood or hickory chips

1 Sprinkle the scallops on both sides with the salt and place on a rack set over a shallow tray or plate. Place the tray, unwrapped, in a part of the refrigerator with cold air circulating. Leave for about 8 hours.
2 Line the bottom of the smoker with aluminum foil and add the wood chips. Set the rack over the chips, place the scallops and fish on top, cover with the lid and turn the heat to high. When the wood chips start to smoke, reduce the heat to low and smoke for about 30 minutes with the lid on. If the wood chips burn out, add more as needed. When the fish and scallops turn light brown, transfer them to a serving plate.

Salt the scallops and dry them out in the refrigerator.

SMOKED CHORIZO SAUSAGE

Handmade chorizo is unbelievably delicious. Just enjoy the plump texture and the tasty, meaty juices that just burst forth from the sausage.

SERVES 4-6

1 salted sheep sausage casing, about 6½ feet (2 m) long
Herbs of your choice (flat-leaf parsley, thyme, rosemary, etc.), to taste
1 oz (30 g) cherrywood or hickory chips

FOR THE FILLING

1 lb (500 g) coarsely ground pork
1 clove garlic, minced
1 tablespoon white wine
1½ teaspoons sea salt
1 teaspoon fennel seeds
1 teaspoon sweet paprika powder
½ teaspoon coarsely ground black pepper
Dash cayenne pepper

1 Soak the sausage casing in water for one hour to remove the salt.
2 Put all the filling ingredients in a large bowl and mix. Attach a ½-in (12-mm) diameter metal sausage filling nozzle on a piping bag. (It's best to reserve the bag for making chorizo only since it will absorb some of the filling odors.)
3 Cover the nozzle with one end of the sausage casing. Fill the casing slowly, leaving about 1 in (3 cm) of the end un-filled. When the casing is filled, twist and tie off both ends.
4 Line the bottom of the smoker with aluminum foil and add the wood chips. Set the rack, place the chorizo on top, cover with the lid and turn the heat on to high. When the wood chips start to smoke, reduce heat to low and smoke for about 30 minutes with the lid on. If the wood chips burn out, add more as needed.
5 When the sausage looks nice and brown, transfer to a serving platter and garnish with the herbs.

Soak the sausage casing to remove the salt.

Fill the sausage casing slowly so that it doesn't burst.

Arrange the chorizo in a spiral, working from the inside out, before placing in the smoker.

SMOKING VEGETABLES, CHEESE, NUTS and OTHER INGREDIENTS

You'll be surprised at what you can smoke, and how much smoking enhances the flavor. Here are just a few ideas to get you started.

HOW TO SMOKE

Line the bottom of the smoker or wok with aluminum foil and put in about 1 oz (30 g) of cherrywood or other chips. Set the rack, place the food to be smoked on top, cover with the lid and turn the heat to high. When the wood chips start to smoke, reduce the heat to low and allow the food to smoke. If the wood chips burn out, add more as needed.

1. TAKUAN PICKLED DAIKON

Takuan is daikon radish that has been pickled using rice bran, salt and various flavoring ingredients like kombu seaweed. Some types of takuan are dyed yellow with turmeric. You can buy takuan at Japanese grocery stores

Smoke a 5-in (12-cm) length of takuan for about 15 minutes. Turn and smoke on the other side for another 15 minutes or so.

2. WALNUTS

Place 3 tablespoons of salted walnut kernels on a piece of aluminum foil and smoke for about 30 minutes.

3. BOILED EGGS

1 Put 3 eggs with enough water to cover in a pan over medium heat. When the water comes to a boil, reduce heat to low and cook for about 8 minutes. Cool in cold water, and peel the eggs.
2 Put 1¾ cups (425 ml) water and 4 teaspoons salt in a bowl and mix. Add the peeled eggs. Cover the bowl with plastic wrap and refrigerate for about an hour. Take the eggs out and pat dry.
3 Smoke for about 15 minutes, turn, and smoke for another 15 minutes.

4. CHEESE

Place 4 oz (125 g) of cheddar or processed cheese on a piece of aluminum foil and smoke for about 30 minutes.

5. ALMONDS

Place ¼ cup (35 g) of salted almonds on a piece of aluminum foil and smoke for about 30 minutes.

Baked Cheesecake
Japanese-style cheesecake is drier and spongier than the creamy Western equivalent). Try smoking a 7-in (18-cm) diameter cheesecake for about 30 minutes.

Chapter 5

THE FINAL COURSE:
RICE, NOODLES and BREAD

The last part of a multi-course meal in Japan—even a leisurely evening of munching and drinking at an izakaya—is called the *shime*, a starchy dish that contains rice, noodles, or bread. After you've had a drink or two, you want to indulge in the satisfaction of a filling, comforting shime. In this chapter you'll find favorites such as Beef Curry Japanese Style; Spicy Fried Rice with Pickled Mustard Greens; and Stir-Fried Udon Noodles with Pork and Root Vegetables. I've also included some unusual dishes like Mackerel Sandwich and Soy Sauce Bruschetta. The shime announces that the meal was a success—and you look forward to the next one.

PICKLED RADISH and GREEN SHISO RICE

Pickled daikon radish is known in Japan as takuan (see page 114). Combined with fragrant green shiso it makes a wonderful rice dish!

SERVES 2

2 green shiso leaves (see note, page 12)
2 cups (400 g) warm cooked rice
1½-in (4-cm) length takuan pickled radish, roughly chopped
1 teaspoon toasted white sesame seeds
Pinch of sea salt, to taste

1 Remove the stems from the shiso leaves. Cut the leaves into four strips and shred finely.
2 Combine the rice in a large bowl with the takuan, shiso, sesame seeds and salt. Mix using a cut and fold motion, then divide between two rice bowls to serve.

CHAZUKE SASHIMI RICE with TEA

Chazuke means rice and other ingredients with hot dashi, green tea or plain hot water poured over. This version features sesame-seasoned sea bream sashimi.

SERVES 2

10 slices sashimi-grade sea bream or other firm white fish (see note, page 102)
2 green shiso leaves (see note, page 12)
2 cups (400 g) warm cooked rice
2 pinches finely shredded nori seaweed*
1¾ cups (425 ml) hot dashi stock (see page 6)
¼ teaspoon wasabi paste

FOR THE MARINADE

1 tablespoon white sesame paste or tahini
2 teaspoons soy sauce
½ teaspoon mirin (see note, page 11)
½ teaspoon sake

*To shred a sheet of nori seaweed, cut it very thinly with kitchen scissors. You can also buy pre-shredded nori at a well-stocked Japanese grocery store.

1 Mix the marinade ingredients in a bowl. Add the sea bream slices and coat with the marinade. Cover with plastic wrap and refrigerate for about 10 minutes.
2 Remove the stems from the shiso leaves, cut the leaves in half lengthwise and shred finely.
3 Divide the rice between two rice bowls and top with the sea bream, shiso and shredded nori seaweed. Add wasabi paste to each bowl and pour equal amounts of hot dashi stock over all.

BEEF CURRY JAPANESE STYLE

A little time and effort will turn a cheap cut of beef into a delicious dish. If you make it in advance and have it in on hand, you can enjoy it quickly and easily whenever you like.

SERVES 4

1 lb (450 g) beef tendon, or brisket
2¾ cups (700 ml) water
1 plain black tea bag
2 onions
1 carrot
1 tablespoon unsalted butter
1 knob fresh ginger, peeled and minced
1 clove garlic, grated
1½ teaspoons sea salt, or to taste
2 tablespoons curry powder
2 tablespoons flour
3½ tablespoons sake
½ cup (125 g) canned diced tomatoes
½ teaspoon soy sauce
4 cups (800 g) warm cooked rice

1 Cut the beef tendon into bite-sized pieces, place in a pan with the water, and turn the heat to high. Just before the water comes to a full boil, skim off the scum and reduce the heat to low. Add the tea bag to the pot, wrapping the string of the tea bag to the pan handle. Simmer for about 1 hour, then remove the tea bag.

2 Finely chop one of the onions (see page 7), and cut the other one into 8 wedges. Peel the carrot and cut it up roughly (see page 6).

3 Melt the butter in a frying pan over low heat. Add the chopped onion, minced ginger and garlic, add the salt and sauté for about 5 minutes. When the onion is lightly browned, add the curry powder and stir. Add the flour and sauté.

4 When the flour in the frying pan no longer looks dry and floury, raise the heat to medium and add the sake and canned tomatoes. Bring to a boil, then turn the heat off.

5 Measure the liquid that was used to simmer the beef in step 1, and add water as needed to bring the total up to 2 cups (500 ml). Return the liquid to the beef pan. Add the contents of the frying pan, the onion wedges and the carrots and bring to a boil over high heat. Turn heat to low and simmer for about 30 minutes. Add the soy sauce and stir. To serve, put some warm cooked rice on a plate and ladle curry over it.

FRIED RICE with SALTED SQUID

The saltiness and pungency of the preserved squid are a great foil for the egg.

SERVES 2

6 oz (170 g) ika no shiokara salted squid*
2 eggs
1 tablespoon vegetable oil
2 cups (400 g) warm cooked rice
2 green onions (scallions), green parts only,
    sliced into thin rounds

*Ika no shiokara This is whole squid – guts and all – fermented and preserved in salt. Ika no shiokara is funky, salty and packed with umami. Once you get accustomed to the taste, you may find it quite addictive. It's sold in jars at Japanese grocery stores. If you can't find it, substitute 3–4 salted anchovies, chopped.

1 Cut the shiokara into tiny pieces. Beat the eggs in a bowl.
2 Heat the oil in a frying pan over medium heat. Add the eggs, then add the rice and stir-fry for about a minute. When the rice grains are separate, make a well in the center, add the chopped-up shiokara and stir-fry quickly. When it is heated through, transfer to two plates. Top with the sliced green onion.

WHITEBAIT and UME RICE BALLS

This dish is made with chirimenjako, tiny semi-dried whitebait that are salted and often mixed with other ingredients like sansho pepper. You can find them in the refrigerated or frozen food section of a Japanese grocery store. Here, the soy sauce enhances the umami of the chirimenjako and the piquancy of the umeboshi pickled plum.

MAKES 2 RICE BALLS

6 small crunchy type (kari-kari) umeboshi (see note,
    page 12)
½ cup (120 g) warm cooked rice
2 tablespoons chirimenjako (see note, above)
½ teaspoon soy sauce

1 Cut the flesh of the umeboshi off the pits and discard the pits.
2 Put the rice, chirimenjako, umeboshi and soy sauce in a large bowl and fold together. Divide into two portions. Wet your hands lightly and shape each portion into a triangular rice ball. Place on a serving plate.

EEL and EGG RICE BOWL

In this classic donburi rice bowl, hot rice is topped with salty-sweet simmered eel and enrobed in a soft-set omelette. The key is to add the beaten egg in two batches. The first batch sets the eel, and the second gives the topping a soft, silky texture. Sansho pepper, which you can find in your Japanese grocery store, adds subtle citrus notes.

SERVES 2

One package eel kabayaki,* about
    6 oz (170 g)
4 eggs
½ onion
2 cups (400 g) warm cooked rice
Dash sansho pepper
A few leaves of mitsuba (Japanese
    parsley) or flat-leaf parsley

FOR THE SIMMERING LIQUID

1 scant cup (200 ml) dashi stock
    (see page 6)
4 teaspoons soy sauce
2 teaspoons mirin (see note, page 11)
2 teaspoons sake

*Kabayaki is eel ready-cooked in a salty-sweet sauce.
It can be found frozen at Japanese grocery stores.

1 Place the eel on baking sheet lined with foil. Bake in the oven preheated to 400°F (200°C) for about 3 minutes.
Slice in half lengthwise, then cut into ¾-in (2-cm) wide pieces.
2 Beat 2 of the eggs in a bowl. Cut the onion into 8 wedges.
3 Bring the simmering liquid ingredients to a boil in a pan over medium heat. When it boils, add the onion, simmer briefly and take the pan off the heat.
4 Divide the warm rice between 2 large bowls. To make the first bowl, place half of the simmered onion and liquid in a small frying pan over medium heat. When the liquid comes to a boil, add half of the eel pieces.
5 Bring the liquid in the frying pan back to a boil, then add half beaten egg from step 2. Simmer while mixing with a fork for about 30 seconds. When the egg is soft set, add the rest of the beaten egg and simmer for about 30 seconds. Add some mitsuba leaves and sprinkle with sansho pepper. Beat the remaining 2 eggs and repeat with the rest of the ingredients to make the other bowl.

MINI KIMBAP KOREAN SUSHI

Roll up this Korean-style sushi and pop it in
your mouth!

MAKES 4 SUSHI ROLLS

4 slices roast pork or char siu (store-bought,
  or see the recipe headnote on page 107 to
  make your own)
A few leaves of kimchi
Handful radish sprouts
1 sheet toasted nori seaweed
Sesame oil, for brushing
Pinch of sea salt
1 cup (200 g) warm cooked rice

1 Cut the roast pork into ¼-in (6-mm) wide strips.
Cut the kimchi into ¾-in (2-cm) wide strips. Cut
the roots off the radish sprouts. Cut the nori sheet
into quarters.
2 Brush the nori squares lightly with sesame oil
and sprinkle with the pinch of sea salt. Divide the
rice between the nori pieces, top with the radish
sprouts, kimchi and roast pork, and transfer to a
serving plate.

EGG and RICE CONGEE

The savor and just-right saltiness of the dashi stock
and the fluffy egg are really pleasing to the taste buds.

SERVES 2

1½ cups (300 g) warm or cold cooked rice
2 eggs
1 green onion (scallion), green part only, sliced diagonally

FOR THE SIMMERING LIQUID
1¾ cups (425 ml) cups dashi stock (see page 6)
2 teaspoons soy sauce
1 teaspoon sea salt, or to taste
Dash of mirin (see note, page 11)

1 Rinse the rice in a colander under running water
and drain. This will keep the rice grains from clumping
together. Beat the eggs in a bowl.
2 Bring the simmering liquid ingredients to a boil in a pan
over medium heat. Add the rinsed rice and return to a
boil. Swirl in the beaten egg, turn the heat down to low
and simmer for about 1 minute. When the egg is soft set,
transfer the porridge to serving bowls and top with the
sliced green onion.

SPICY FRIED RICE with PICKLED MUSTARD GREENS

You'll find the spicy takanazuke pickled mustard greens at your local Japanese grocery store, where it's usually sold as a whole leaf. Takanazuke adds a great layer of umami to the nutty sesame oil and spicy chili.

SERVES 2

3 oz (85 g) pickled mustard greens (takanazuke)*
½ onion
½ red Thai chili pepper, or to taste
2 eggs
1 tablespoon sesame oil
2 cups (400 g) cooked rice
½ teaspoon soy sauce

*If you can't find takanazuke at your Japanese grocery store, you may be able to get hold of zha cai, Chinese pickled kohlrabi, which has the same salty mustardy flavor as takanazuke.

1 Chop the takanazuke roughly. Finely chop the onion (see page 7). Deseed the chili pepper and slice thinly.
2 Beat the eggs in a bowl. Heat half of the sesame oil in a frying pan over medium heat. Add the beaten eggs and scramble them until soft set. Transfer to a separate bowl.
3 Wipe out the frying pan and heat the remaining sesame oil over medium heat. Add the chopped takanazuke and stir-fry for about 30 seconds. When it becomes fragrant, add the onion and chili pepper and stir-fry for another minute or so.
4 When all the contents of the pan are well coated in sesame oil, add the rice and the scrambled egg and stir-fry some more. When the rice grains have separated, turn off the heat, add the soy sauce and mix well. Distribute between two serving plates.

Mix well as you stir-fry so the flavor of the sesame oil is transferred to the takanazuke.

UDON SOUP with MIZUNA GREENS

Mizuna greens lend a fresh light flavor to this dish.

SERVES 2

Small bunch mizuna greens or watercress,
    roots removed, cut into 2-in (5-cm) lengths
1 knob fresh ginger, peeled and minced
2 pinches bonito flakes (see note, page 11)
1/2 teaspoon soy sauce
2 packets fresh or frozen udon noodles*

FOR THE SOUP
2 1/2 cups (625 ml) dashi stock (see page 6)
2 tablespoons mirin (see note, page 11)
2 tablespoons soy sauce
1/4 teaspoon sea salt, or to taste

*You can use 6 oz (170 g) dried udon instead. Cook as directed on the package, drain, and rinse in cold running water. Then follow the recipe.

1 Put the mizuna in a bowl with the ginger and bonito flakes. Add the soy sauce and mix lightly.
2 Put the soup ingredients in a pan over medium heat and bring to a boil. Add the noodles and cook for the time stated on the packet. Divide the udon noodles and soup between two bowls and top with the seasoned mizuna from step 1.

SOBA NOODLE and TOMATO SALAD

Buckwheat soba noodles get an Italian touch!

SERVES 2

2 large ripe tomatoes
1 tablespoon olive oil
1 clove garlic, thinly sliced
1 red Thai chili pepper, deseeded
1/4 red onion, thinly sliced
1 teaspoon sea salt, or to taste
8 oz (225 g) fresh soba noodles*
6 leaves frilly loose-leaf lettuce, torn into bite-sized pieces

*If you can't find fresh soba noodles, cook 4 oz (125 g) dried soba noodles as directed on the package.

1 Cut the tomatoes into 8 wedges, then cut each wedge in half crosswise.
2 Saute the garlic in the olive oil over low heat for 3 minutes until lightly browned. Add the chili pepper, heat briefly in the oil, then transfer the contents of the pan to a large bowl and let cool. Add the tomatoes and onion and mix.
3 Bring a large pot of water to a boil and add the salt. Add the soba and cook as directed on the package. Rinse in cold water and drain. Add the noodles to the bowl in step 2 and mix. Line two serving plates with the lettuce and divide the noodle salad between them.

SEA URCHIN SPAGHETTI CARBONARA

The richness of the preserved sea urchin combined with the fresh cream is exceptional. The rich and yummy taste is enhanced by sautéed bacon and liberal amounts of freshly ground black pepper.

SERVES 2

3 slices thick-cut bacon
Scant ½ cup (100 ml) heavy cream
2 tablespoons preserved sea urchin
  (shio uni, sold in jars at Japanese
  grocery stores)*
5 oz (140 g) uncooked spaghetti
1 tablespoon sea salt, or to taste
Coarsely ground black pepper, to
  taste

*If you can't find shio uni, any sort of fish roe, such as mentaiko, salmon or tobiko roe, can be used instead.

1 Set a large pot of water to a boil over high heat.
2 Cut the bacon into ¼ x 1½ in (5 mm x 4 cm) pieces. Place in a frying pan over medium heat and sauté for about 2 minutes. When the fat begins to render out and the bacon is lightly browned, add the cream, then the preserved sea urchin, mixing after each addition. Take the pan off the heat.
3 When the water in the large pot has reached a boil, add the salt. Add the spaghetti and cook as directed on the package. Reserve ½ cup (125 ml) of the pasta water before draining.
4 Return the frying pan with the sauce to medium heat. Drain the spaghetti and immediately mix it in with the sauce in the frying pan. Add some of the reserved pasta water to thin the sauce if needed. Divide the spaghetti between two serving plates and sprinkle coarsely ground black pepper on top.

As soon as the spaghetti is cooked and drained, add it to the frying pan ingredients and mix.

RAMEN with SPICY GROUND PORK DIPPING SAUCE

A key ingredient in this dish is doubanjiang, a fermented paste from China made with broad beans, soy beans, salt, rice and spices. It is used to add heat and umami to various dishes. You'll find it at Asian or Chinese grocery stores. In Japanese grocery stores it's called tobanjan.

SERVES 2

2 hard-boiled eggs
1 cup (100 g) bean sprouts
1 tablespoon sesame oil
½ teaspoon minced garlic
1 teaspoon doubanjiang (see note, above)
5 oz (140 g) ground pork
14 oz (400 g) fresh Chinese noodles*
4-in (10-cm) length green onion (scallion)
    (white part only), thinly sliced

FOR THE SAUCE
⅔ cup (160 ml) dashi stock (see page 6)
4 teaspoons tahini
2 teaspoons miso paste
2 teaspoons soy sauce

*Chinese Noodles If you can't find fresh Chinese noodles at your grocery store, use thin dried spaghetti instead.

1 Peel the boiled eggs and cut into 4 wedges. Remove the roots and caps from the bean sprouts, then blanch for about 30 seconds in boiling water. Drain.
2 Combine the Sauce ingredients in a bowl and mix well.
3 Heat the sesame oil in a frying pan over medium heat. Add the garlic and doubanjiang and stir-fry for about 30 seconds. When the pan starts to smell fragrant, add the pork and stir-fry for about 3 minutes.
4 When the pork changes color, add the dipping sauce and mix. When the pan comes to a boil, lower the heat and simmer for 2 minutes. Pour into two serving bowls.
5 Bring a pan of water to a boil. Add the noodles and cook following the packet instructions. (If your noodles didn't come with instructions, boil them for about 3 minutes, then test a strand; boil for another minute or so if needed.) Drain the noodles and rinse while rubbing under cold running water. Drain again, and distribute onto two plates. Top with the eggs, bean sprouts and green onion.

When the doubanjiang, garlic and sesame oil start to give off a fragrance, add the meat.

STIR-FRIED UDON NOODLES with PORK and ROOT VEGETABLES

Fish sauce gives a Southeast Asian twist.

SERVES 2

- 2 portions fresh or frozen udon wheat noodles (see note, page 122)
- 1-in (3-cm) piece lotus root, about 2 oz (60 g) (see note, page 11)
- ¼ medium carrot
- 6-in (15-cm) length Japanese or baby leek, or thick green onion (white part only)
- 1 tablespoon vegetable oil
- 4 oz (125 g) thinly sliced pork belly (store-bought, or see recipe headnote on page 107 to make your own)
- 4 green onions (scallions), green parts only, sliced into 1-in (3-cm) lengths
- 2 tablespoons fish sauce
- Dash of black pepper

1 If using frozen udon, defrost in the microwave following the packet instructions.
2 Peel the lotus root and slice into thin rounds. Rinse in a colander under running water and drain. Peel the carrot and slice into half-moons. Slice the leek diagonally into ½-in (1-cm) wide pieces.
3 Heat the vegetable oil in a frying pan over medium heat. Add the pork belly and stir-fry until it changes color, then add the vegetables from step 2 and stir. Add the fresh or defrosted udon noodles and the green onions, untangling the noodles. Add the fish sauce and pepper, stir briefly, and serve.

SAKURA SHRIMP PASTA

Sakura shrimp are tiny pinkish-red dried shrimp, usually sold in Japanese grocery stores. They add wonderful umami and texture to a dish.

SERVES 2

- 1 tablespoon sea salt, or to taste
- 5 oz (140 g) uncooked spaghetti
- 1 clove garlic
- 4 tablespoons olive oil, divided
- 1 red Thai chili pepper, deseeded and chopped
- 4 tablespoons dried sakura shrimp (see note, above)

1 Bring plenty of water to boil in a large pot with the salt. Add the spaghetti and cook as directed on the package. Reserve ½ cup (125 ml) of the cooking water before draining. Mince the garlic clove finely (see page 7).
2 Heat 2 tablespoons of the olive oil in a frying pan over low heat. Add the garlic and chili pepper and stir-fry for about 2 minutes.
3 Take the pan off the heat and add the sakura shrimp and 2 tablespoons of the reserved pasta water. Return the pan to medium heat, add the drained cooked spaghetti and mix in the remaining 2 tablespoons of olive oil. Serve.

SHRIMP TOAST

Salt lightly so the sweetness of the shrimp shines through. Enjoy the crispy goodness of this delicious snack when it's piping hot.

SERVES 2

1 slice thick-cut toast bread*
8 small fresh shrimp in their shells, about 4 oz (125 g) total
¼ teaspoon sea salt, or to taste
1 clove garlic, minced
Pinch of black pepper
Oil for deep-frying

*The thick-cut toast bread used here is about 1-in (3-cm) thick. You can use white bread sliced for Texas toast, although this is usually a little thinner. To duplicate the original recipe, buy a loaf of "4-slice bread" at a Japanese bakery, or get an unsliced loaf and slice it thickly yourself.

1 Cut the crusts off the bread and roll it out thinly with a rolling pin.
2 Peel the shrimp and remove the veins. Chop them up first, then go over them again with a knife to chop them into a paste.
3 Combine the chopped shrimp, garlic, salt and pepper in a bowl and mix well with a spoon. Spread on one side of the bread.
4 Heat the frying oil to 355°F (180°C). Place the bread shrimp-side-down in the oil and fry for about 2 minutes, until it starts to brown. Flip over and fry for another minute or so. Take the bread out and drain off the oil. Cut into 4 squares and arrange on a serving plate.

Roll the rolling pin back and forth firmly to flatten the bread.

SOY SAUCE BRUSCHETTA

Brush some soy sauce on toasted baguette slices, sprinkle with sugar and toast again. It's so simple, yet so good.

SERVES 2

½ baguette, about 4-in (10-cm) long
1 teaspoon soy sauce
1 teaspoon sugar

1 Preheat oven to 355°F (180°C). Slice the baguette into ¼-in (6-mm) thick diagonal slices. Line a baking sheet with parchment paper and place the baguette slices on it. Bake for about 10 minutes to dry out the baguette.
2 Lightly brush one side of each slice with soy sauce and sprinkle with sugar. Return to oven for another 5 minutes, then remove and arrange on a serving plate.

MACKEREL SANDWICH

This surprisingly delicious sandwich is a new discovery for me. It's my version of a sandwich that originates from Turkey.

SERVES 2

1 piece baguette, about 8-in (20-cm) long
1 semi-dried mackerel, about 4 oz (125 g)*
1 lettuce leaf, torn into pieces
1 tablespoon mayonnaise

*The semi-dried mackerel used here (called bunka-boshi) is fresh mackerel that has been salted, then dried with cold air indoors. You may be able to find this at a well-stocked Japanese grocery store. If you can get some very fresh mackerel, make your own bunka-boshi by filleting and cleaning it, patting it dry, salting it generously on both sides, then refrigerating it for 8–10 hours.

1 Slice the baguette in half lengthwise. Place in the oven preheated to 400°F (200°C) with the cut side up and toast for about 3 minutes.
2 Debone the mackerel. Heat a frying pan over medium-low heat, place the mackerel in it skin side down, and pan-fry for about 3 minutes. When the skin is lightly browned, flip the fish over and pan-fry for another minute or so.
3 Spread the cut sides of the toasted baguette with the mayonnaise. Place some of the lettuce on once half and top with the mackerel. Cover with the other half of the baguette, cut in half and arrange on a serving plate.

Published by Tuttle Publishing, an imprint of
Periplus Editions (HK) Ltd.

www.tuttlepublishing.com

DANSHI CHUBO IZAKAYA RYORI by Wataru Yokota
Copyright © SEIBIDO SHUPPAN 2015
English translation © 2019 Periplus Editions (HK) Ltd.
All rights reserved.
Original Japanese edition published by SEIBIDO
SHUPPAN Co., Ltd.

Photographs © Hidetoshi Hara

This English edition is published by arrangement with
SEIBIDO SHUPPAN Co., Ltd., Tokyo in care of
Tuttle-Mori Agency, Inc., Tokyo.

English translation by Makiko Itoh.

Photos page 4 from left to right: Yulia Grigoryeva;
Rei Imagine; Wuttisit Somtui; all Shutterstock.com

ISBN: 978-4-8053-1528-6

26 25 24 23
10 9 8 7 6 5 4

Printed in China   2312EP

DISTRIBUTED BY

North America, Latin America & Europe
Tuttle Publishing
364 Innovation Drive
North Clarendon, VT 05759-9436 U.S.A.
Tel: 1 (802) 773 8930
Fax: 1 (802) 773 6993
info@tuttlepublishing.com
www.tuttlepublishing.com

Japan
Tuttle Publishing
Yaekari Building 3rd Floor
5-4-12 Osaki
Shinagawa-ku
Tokyo 141-0032
Tel: (81) 3 5437 0171
Fax: (81) 3 5437 0755
sales@tuttle.co.jp
www.tuttle.co.jp

Asia Pacific
Berkeley Books Pte. Ltd.
3 Kallang Sector #04-01,
Singapore 349278
Tel: (65) 6741 2178
Fax: (65) 6741 2179
inquiries@periplus.com.sg
www.tuttlepublishing.com

TUTTLE PUBLISHING® is a registered trademark
of Tuttle Publishing, a division of Periplus Editions
(HK) Ltd.

"Books to Span the East and West"

Tuttle Publishing was founded in 1832 in the small New England town of Rutland, Vermont
[USA]. Our core values remain as strong today as they were then—to publish best-in-class books
which bring people together one page at a time. In 1948, we established a publishing outpost in
Japan—and Tuttle is now a leader in publishing English-language books about the arts, languages
and cultures of Asia. The world has become a much smaller place today and Asia's economic
and cultural influence has grown. Yet the need for meaningful dialogue and information about
this diverse region has never been greater. Over the past seven decades, Tuttle has published
thousands of books on subjects ranging from martial arts and paper crafts to language learning
and literature—and our talented authors, illustrators, designers and photographers have won
many prestigious awards. We welcome you to explore the wealth of information available on Asia
at **www.tuttlepublishing.com**.